VICTIM
AFTERSHOCK

VICTIM AFTER-SHOCK

HOW TO GET RESULTS FROM THE CRIMINAL JUSTICE SYSTEM

JUDGE JAMES E. MORRIS

FRANKLIN WATTS
New York | London | Toronto | Sydney
1983

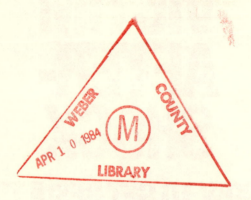

Library of Congress Cataloging in Publication Data

Morris, James E.
Victim aftershock.

Includes index.
1. Criminal justice, Administration of—United States.
2. Victims of crimes—United States. I. Title.
KF9223.M646   1983   344.73'03288   82-24844
ISBN 0-531-09891-5   347.3043288
ISBN 0-531-09954-7 (pbk.)

ACKNOWLEDGMENTS

Once the decision to write this book was made, I needed much assistance and encouragement, which was freely given. I am especially grateful to the public officials on both sides of the bench throughout the criminal justice system, who gave me helpful ideas and different perspectives; to all the victims who agreed to discuss their misfortunes; to my research assistants, Michelle D'Ambrosia and Thomas Bolon, who provided the necessary backup material and extensive, precise research; to Sharon Camarata-Konrad of the Victims' Assistance Unit of the Rochester, New York, Police Department who gave me much insight and direction; to my friend Kenneth A. Whitman of the Garden Grove, California, Police Department for encouragement and advice; to the officials of the National Organization for Victims' Assistance in Washington, D.C., for their overview; to Vicki Brown for her preliminary editorial work, performed with the highest professional expertise; and to Liz Hock, my editor, and Arthur Pine and Richard Pine, my literary agents, for the confidence they have placed in this project.

To my secretary Carol Russo, for her determination in making sure that I made all deadlines by typing the manuscript in record time; to my friends, Josephine D'Ambrosia and Virginia Bergan, whose personal support has been more meaningful than they will ever know; and most especially to my daughters, Kim and Debbie, for being so very patient with me for taking time away from their time to write this book, I give my heartfelt thanks.

NOTE

The information contained herein is based upon Judge Morris' experiences as a former assistant district attorney, defense attorney, and judge. More than 100 interviews of people who work in the criminal justice system and victims were conducted. Although the cases are real, the names used in the examples are fictitious. Real names have been used in those instances where cases have received national recognition. Statistical data was obtained from the Federal Bureau of Investigation, Uniform Crime Reports of 1981, *Crime in the United States*, released to the public August 26, 1982.

CONTENTS

Chapter 7
Rape 101

What to Do If You Are Attacked
What to Do If You Are Raped
Compensation for Injuries
Avoiding Rape
Rape Crisis Services
New Attitudes Benefit Rape Victims

Chapter 8
Property Crimes 117

Burglary
The Financial Loss
The Emotional Upset
When You Discover a Burglary
Other Problems Burglary Victims Face
Additional Problems

Larceny-Theft
Bicycle Thefts
Stolen Motor Vehicles
Credit Card Thefts
Bad Checks

Vandalism

Chapter 9
Crimes Committed in the Use of a Motor Vehicle 141

Driving While Intoxicated
How Much Is Legally Drunk
The Arrest of the Drunken Driver
Defendants Have Many Rights

VICTIM
AFTERSHOCK

PREFACE

The wrongful acts of others—crimes against persons, crimes against property, and the so-called victimless crimes—affect us all. In 1981, according to a recent Justice Department report, 30 percent of the nation's households were touched by crime. Another report provides the grim statistics that 41 million individuals became victims through completed or attempted offenses. Yet despite the large and shocking numbers, the unflagging media coverage, and the increasingly strong response from both individuals and communities, one integral aspect of crime is usually overlooked: the victim. All too often it is the victim's fate to become lost within the criminal justice system or simply forgotten. As if the disruption, destruction, and sadness that stains a victim's life is not devastating enough, a second bout of victimization occurs when those who administer law and justice do not respond to the victim's needs.

Victim aftershock, the inability of victims to achieve satisfaction through the criminal justice system, prompted me to write this book. With adequate preparation and knowledge of the criminal justice system, victim aftershock can be countered by victims who work through the system to achieve the results that they want.

In the pages that follow you will learn about the types of crimes—personal crimes of violence (rape, murder, and mugging), property crimes, burglary, theft, and vandalism, family crimes (battered spouse, child abuse, and incest), motor vehicle crimes (driving while intoxicated), and victimless crimes (prostitution and gambling)—and the types of punishment. It should be noted, however, that the purpose here is not to recount horror stories but to focus on the aftereffects of crimes—the losses, the agonies, the frustrations, the inconveniences—and to identify various ways a victim might achieve positive results. Success stories of victims who have managed to be heard and who have obtained the results they sought buttress the text.

You will also learn about the criminal justice system: what it constitutes, what to expect from it, how to avoid being victimized by it. Police, judges, and prosecutors are receptive to your thoughts and concerns and want to satisfy your needs. Unless you initiate contact with the proper person in the criminal justice system, however, your case will be handled routinely. Procedures are presented step by step to facilitate your dealing with the system, and your most basic questions (for example, *How many times must I go to court? Can property that has been recovered be returned?*) have been anticipated and addressed.

The little publicized, but widely available, methods of victim compensation and restitution are fully explained. Appendix A provides a detailed listing of victims' compensation programs in thirty-eight states, and Appendix B provides 141 rape crisis service hotline numbers for 126 cities. There is also a glossary.

The single most effective way to prevent victim aftershock, of course, is crime prevention, and this is a recurring theme of *Victim Aftershock*.

It is my intention and hope that, armed with the information and insights presented here, you will increase your chances of being successful in the criminal justice system, you should no longer fear getting involved, your expectations should be reasonable and realistic, and you should be equipped to prevent victim aftershock.

James E. Morris
February, 1983

PART I
THE PEOPLE AND THE SYSTEM

CHAPTER 1
THE SYSTEM

You are a woman walking down a familiar street, a street that has always seemed safe. Suddenly you are grabbed from behind. You resist. A tussle ensues. Your screams finally scare off your assailant. You have not been harmed, you have avoided possible assault, and you breathe a great sigh of relief. You are, however, a victim.

What should you do? Is there anything you can do? You feel you must do something. You contact the police, you get involved, and you worry: Will the system really help me?

Arriving home from work, you find your home ransacked. Shocked, you reach for your telephone and dial the police. They arrive quickly and begin dusting for fingerprints. The officer in charge asks endless questions. You are left with rather a mess to clean up, and you have suffered considerable financial loss. Much worse, how-

ever, is the emotional trauma initiated by the invasion of your privacy. Months pass. You wonder if the authorities will ever contact you. You wonder if the intruder has been caught. You wonder if you will ever hear of the incident again.

Your car is legally parked in front of your home. You hear a crash and run outside in time to see another car pulling away. Quickly, you call the police, giving them the license number of the second car. After several minutes, an overworked, tired but sympathetic police officer arrives and seats himself at your kitchen table. He questions you and writes down your age, your place of employment, and other personal information about you. You are impatient and frustrated. This is the last you hear from the police.

These are typical of events that happen thousands of times each day in the United States. Some 1.3 million violent crimes were reported to police agencies in 1981. In addition, there were 4 million burglaries, 7 million larceny-thefts, and more than 1 million motor vehicle thefts reported. An untold number of incidents involving vandalism and petty offenses occurred. Nearly one-half of all crimes are never reported, often because the victim is afraid to get involved or because he or she believes that nothing can be done.

Shock, trauma, disbelief, and fear are conditions that usually attend your becoming a victim. You feel completely disoriented, that your life is swirling about you, that you have lost control.

Your lack of knowledge about what *really* happens when you call the police may prompt feelings of intimidation. Images flash in your mind of repeated questioning by police officers, the district attorney, and the defense attorney. You may feel a sense of helplessness, and you may fear reprisal. Perhaps the media have caused you to be wary of the criminal justice system. Or, you may expect too much because you believe that good always triumphs over evil, that the police always apprehend and arrest offenders.

Whereas federal law enforcement agencies investigate violations involving federal law, state and local police maintain safety and enforce laws that most directly affect an individual's everyday life. Generally, when you are victimized, you will be dealing only with local and state officials, laws and courts.

There are many capable people in law enforcement throughout the country. They respond to, and investigate, crimes, arrest and prosecute offenders, and work to prevent crime. Judges, district attorneys, probation officers, parole officers, police, clerks, and others in the system are well intentioned and often well trained. However, most of them, especially in the larger, urban areas, are overworked; enormous case loads pressure them to go on to the next case, interview the next client, finish their docket. As a result, they may unintentionally rate the satisfaction of the victim a low priority. This is particularly unfortunate. Crime takes many forms, and the results are invariably traumatic.

Survivors of crimes of personal violence—rape, attempted murder, mugging—suffer both the initial trauma

and deep and lasting emotional scars—flashbacks of the
crime, and a fear of never having a normal life again. In
addition, there is secondary injury to family members.
Offenses between members of a family—battered spouse,
child abuse, incest—are of great concern not only to the
family but to the criminal justice system, which deals
sensitively with such tragedies. The drunken driver often
leaves a path of heartache: the destruction of innocent
people who just happened to be in the wrong place at the
wrong time.

On a different level, property crimes involving theft,
vandalism, and shoplifting result in not only financial
loss but annoyance, inconvenience, and disruption. The
so-called victimless crimes of prostitution and gambling
can lead to serious consequences, creating many more
victims than one might suspect.

All these crimes deserve to be dealt with positively
and directly by the criminal justice system.

WHO GETS THE ATTENTION—
DEFENDANT OR VICTIM?

A youth snatches a purse. When he is apprehended and
arrested, all the attention of the criminal justice system
is focused on him. Extensive support services are made
available to him. If necessary, an attorney can be supplied
by the Legal Aid Society or the Public Defender's Office,
often free of charge. Social agencies and well-meaning
individuals attempt to help defendants who are poor and

downtrodden, as well as members of the defendant's family. These groups and individuals work for pretrial release, social programs, rehabilitation programs, and reeducation.

Thousands and even tens of thousands of dollars can be spent on an individual defendant. All this interest, attention, and money benefits the person who is accused of committing a violation against another person.

A defendant's rights are supported by the law and financial resources, but the person whose life is affected most severely and directly by a criminal act is often forgotten. There is no discrimination where victims are concerned. Young or old, educated or uneducated, with or without means, selected intentionally or at random— from the moment a person becomes a victim, he or she becomes a second-class citizen. After the initial police reports, the victim becomes faceless and often nameless. All criminal prosecutions are conducted in the name of the *People of the State* v. *a named defendant* (who has the spotlight of the hour).

Victims often suffer financial and personal losses beyond the crime itself because of the demands the system places on them. They may feel that they are not understood, that their position is not explained, that no one acts in their behalf. Victims often miss time at work and experience personal inconvenience, unnecessary anxiety, and degradation. They may be asked the same question over and over by several police officers and different district attorneys; they may be apprehensive about court appearances and fear cross-examination, or they may be treated in what they feel is an indifferent manner by the court. The individual who feels victimized by the criminal justice system suffers from victim aftershock.

VICTIMS CAN BE HEARD

As a victim you should insist on knowing what results you may achieve and on having the opportunity to make your thoughts known to the criminal justice system. You may seek restitution from the offender or a sentence involving community work service. You may want to deter the person from committing the crime again or aid in obtaining rehabilitation or psychiatric service for the defendant. You may want to see the defendant put in jail— or you may merely want to be left alone.

Many persons employed in the criminal justice system forget that everyone in the system is meant to serve others, that victims and witnesses should receive fair, just, and humane treatment. Defendants' rights took center stage in the sixties and seventies, and only now is the plight of the victim beginning to get attention that is long overdue.

The entire scheme of order in our country is based on the cooperation of victims and witnesses with law enforcement authorities. A full understanding of the criminal justice system will enable you to work with authorities in the system and thus avoid being twice victimized.

CHAPTER 2
UNDERSTANDING THE LAW

When was the last time you saw a television newscast that didn't include at least one scene of a handcuffed defendant being escorted to or from a courtroom by three or four police officers? Such scenes may lead you to conclude that the good guys always get the bad guys, that goodness triumphs over evil, and that justice is easily accomplished. In truth, in a majority of crimes, no arrest is made. Of all crimes committed in our country, only one-half are ever reported.

Television newscasts sensationalize and highlight only those cases that are unusual or bizarre. In doing battle in a constant ratings war, news shows compete for a share of the viewing audience. News shows seek to gain your attention; to do so, the producers seem to feel that the show must entertain as well as inform. Excitement is injected into those areas of crime that are savage, and defendants are almost always spotlighted.

Movies and television programs such as *The French Connection*, *Serpico*, *Hill Street Blues*, *Hawaii Five-O*, and *Perry Mason* have been produced for entertainment. Like many news shows, these too have given you a mistaken impression of how the criminal justice system really works.

Alas, the police do not always get their man. Every case is not a thriller. Most details of law enforcement are dull and routine. Your own case is never too unimportant for the police. Courtroom drama produces neither surprise witnesses nor sobbing confessions from the witness stand. The "open file" policy, wherein attorneys disclose their files to one another, makes a surprise virtually impossible.

Neither is the criminal justice system as exciting as that depiction portrayed by the media. It is well organized in a certain definite and logical order and is staffed by men and women who have specific tasks and functions as police, judges, prosecutors, clerks, probation and parole officers, and defense attorneys. Their work is at times repetitious, routine, and frustrating.

For a clearer understanding of the criminal justice system and its people, it is essential that you have some knowledge of the law and the way in which it affects you.

CIVIL AND CRIMINAL LAW

Law itself is a system of principles and rules of human conduct that we must live by and that we expect others to obey. These standards have been framed by the United States Constitution and the constitution of each state. They have been codified and written into specific laws by each state's legislature and approved by the state's chief executive—the governor. They may have been further interpreted by judges in case law.

The law protects you and your property from others and likewise protects others from you. Your life is governed by both civil and criminal law from the day you are born, when a health officer files your birth certificate, until you die, when the death certificate is signed by the attending physician. Although most of what you hear and read concerns criminal law and its sensational aspects, civil law actually makes up more than 90 percent of the written statutory law. Civil law deals with myriad areas: interpreting contracts or relationships between people; determining who's at fault in accident cases; marriages and divorces; child support and custody, and much more. Criminal law deals with those actions that are considered violations against the safety and order of all of us.

Police officers may be considered the troops on the front lines. Your own personal involvement with the police may be limited to the times a flashing red light on a police car has made you pull over to the side of the road. Just as a referee's presence on a football field ensures that the game is played according to the rules, a police officer's job is to ensure the safety of all the members of a community, to be certain that the rules of law are adhered to and enforced. The function of the local police is to keep order, to protect life and property, and to apprehend and arrest people who have violated the law so that the sanctions established in the laws may be imposed.

Police officers are called when your safety has been violated by another person, but they are not employed to enforce civil law. To make clear the difference between civil law and criminal law, consider whether the matter in question is one for the police, that is, a violation against the order of the community and your own personal safety.

A repairman comes to your house and repairs your washing machine. After you give him $35 and he leaves, you find that the machine still does not work properly. Obviously, you don't call the police. The situation does not impair your safety or the safety of the community. A broken washing machine is an inconvenience. The repairman has not honored his contract to provide proper workmanship. You have a case against the repairman, but not in a criminal court; it is a civil contract dispute. You can use Small Claims Court to bring an action in your name against the repairman.

You are involved in a marital dispute and have decided it is time to obtain a divorce, but you don't call a police officer. Instead, you call your lawyer and proceed in the proper court to obtain the relief you seek.

You are involved in an automobile accident. A police officer arrives to help restore order, administer first aid, protect your safety, and direct traffic on the highway, but he will not become involved in any lawsuits that may follow. Who is at fault and who should pay for damages

*either to the automobile or for injuries must be deter-
mined in a civil court.*

*An intruder breaks into your home and carries out money,
a television set, and other items belonging to you. The
intruder's action is a criminal violation against you and
the entire community. The action is both an invasion of
privacy and theft. Call the police.*

*Your purse is snatched as you walk down the street. This
is not a dispute between two people but a criminal action
defined as offensive to the safety and welfare of the entire
community. Purse snatching is robbery. Call the police.*

Disputes involving civil law

- do not involve the police
- do not affect the safety of the entire community
- do not threaten life
- are brought to court on an individual basis, for example, *Smith* v. *Jones*
- involve the use of a private attorney
- are not channeled through the criminal justice system

Disputes involving criminal law

- involve the police
- affect the safety of the entire community   X
- may be dangerous, cause injury, or be life threatening

- are brought to court in the name of the people of the community, for example, *People of the State of New York* v. *Jones*, *State of California* v. *Smith*
- are prosecuted by the district attorney, an official public officer
- are channeled through the criminal justice system following an arrest or indictment

CRIMES AND VIOLATIONS

Criminal law divides crime into two major categories: felonies and misdemeanors. Lesser violations are called petty offenses, violations, and infractions. Although several options are available to courts in sentencing, crimes are classified as either felonies or misdemeanors by the maximum sentences that could be imposed. Felonies, the most serious crimes, are punishable by sentences ranging from more than one year to life in prison or, in some states, the death penalty. Felonies include:
- homicide, manslaughter
- robbery
- assault with a weapon that results in serious injury
- rape
- sex crimes such as sodomy, sexual misconduct, and sexual abuse
- kidnapping
- grand larceny—theft of more than $250
- forgery
- burglary—breaking into a building or home
- arson—setting a fire

- criminal mischief—damage to property of more than $250
- sale of unlawful drugs

Misdemeanors are considered lesser offenses in which the possible maximum prison sentence is one year. Misdemeanors include:

- petty larceny—thefts valued at less than $250, such as shoplifting (the dollar amount may vary in some states)
- simple assault—no weapon is used and there is no serious injury
- criminal mischief—vandalism
- unauthorized use of a vehicle—such as joy riding in a stolen car
- public lewdness
- issuing a bad check
- endangering the welfare of a child
- possession of a weapon (also may be a felony)
- trespass in an enclosed area

Although violations of the law that are primarily nuisances—petty offenses, violations and infractions—are not treated as crimes, they do pass through the local criminal courts. The law does not permit a jury trial in these cases. The maximum sentence possible is less than six months, but often the sentence is only for a few days. Often the judge will only fine or lecture the offender. Petty offenses include:

- disorderly conduct

- harassment
- trespass
- violations of the vehicle and traffic laws
  (except driving while intoxicated; see Chapter 9)
- loitering
- unlawful possession of marijuana

Not all offenses have been listed; the lists above only provide examples in each category.

Offenses can escalate from petty offenses to misdemeanors to felonies. Take the area of trespass, for example. If you walk across your neighbor's yard after he tells you to stay off, you may be guilty of simple trespass, which is a petty offense. If you walk across his lawn and jump over his fence into his backyard, you may be guilty of a misdemeanor because you have entered an area specifically designed to exclude intruders. If, after you jump over the fence, you decide to enter his house without permission, even if you don't break down the door, you may be guilty of a felony burglary, which is the highest form of trespass.

Other crimes become more serious depending on the amount of money or the value of the property involved.

Two brothers walked into an appliance store and decided each would steal a television set. Bill carried out a black and white set worth $199; and Bob took out a small color set worth $410. Although both walked in with the same intention, Bob was charged with a felony. He faced a much more serious sentence than Bill, who was charged with shoplifting, a misdemeanor in that state.

Most violations of the law are prosecuted by the district attorney in accordance with the state penal law or criminal code. Your town, village, or city government may also pass ordinances regulating specific conduct unique to your community, such as unnecessary noise, park regulations, zoning requirements, and dog ordinances. Crimes involving these ordinances are prosecuted by your local government in the local criminal court.

PRIORITIES OF CRIMES

Felonies, the most serious crimes, are treated with a high degree of priority by both the police and the court system. Police have special teams to investigate violent felonies such as murder, armed robbery, and rape. Many departments also have special squads to investigate arson and burglaries. Decoy operations and technical units are often used by these special teams. Police officers will sometimes dress as senior citizens to catch purse snatchers and muggers who prey upon the elderly. Women officers pose as decoys to catch potential rapists. The fingerprinting and laboratory procedures used by the police are usually state of the art equipment. Even infrared cameras and aerial surveillance are used to combat felonies. Finally, hundreds of hours of investigative time may be devoted to a felony in an attempt to solve the case and make an arrest.

The district attorney's office is in charge of prosecuting cases for each county. Each office has a special felony bureau staffed by their most experienced attorneys, and each attorney deals with a specific type of crime. The homicide division, the violent felony offender bureau, and the arson prosecutor, all exist to speed up and stream-line the prosecution of the most serious crimes.

In some states special courts are convened to handle a large number of felony trials. Judges become specialists for a time in a particular criminal court. In New York State recently, hundreds of judges were transferred from civil duties to assist with hearings and trials in the pro-cessing of criminal cases.

Although they are much more numerous than felonies, misdemeanor cases do not routinely get the same priority or attention. Rarely is there a squad to investigate shop-lifting, harassment, or even vandalism. In some areas, police will not respond to delayed reports, that is, a report of a crime after the actual offense has occurred.

WHO DECIDES ON PROSECUTION

The decision to make a felony arrest is usually made by a police officer or the district attorney's office. In all other arrests, the decision to arrest lies with the victim. A police officer or the district attorney rarely seeks to prosecute a misdemeanor or petty offense unless the vic-tim insists that a charge be made. This is especially true in the larger urban areas.

However, misdemeanors and lesser infractions are im-portant if you are the person who has been victimized.

If it is your lawn that has been run over and damaged,
it is your privacy that has been infringed upon. You have
to live with the results. You may want accountability
even though it is a misdemeanor. The person who called
you names and spit at you during an argument may have
committed only a petty offense or infraction, but you are
upset, possibly fearful, and your day is ruined. In the
overall system, however, misdemeanors and violations
of this type have very low priority. The most serious
problem for the entire community are repeaters, or re-
cidivists, involved in felonies. Budget and time con-
straints require that prosecutors and judges concentrate
on those crimes that most affect the community.   *Felony*

To obtain accountability for misdemeanors and lesser
infractions, you must take the initiative. Ask about alternatives to arrest available in the criminal justice system. Such alternatives include centers for dispute
settlement, pretrial diversion, arbitration, and mediation.

Although you have been victimized, your situation will
not be a priority to those in the system unless the crime
is a felony. Therefore, unless you show continued interest
in prosecution, your case will be dismissed for lack of
interest. When you make your priorities known, they
become the priorities of those who serve you.

CHAPTER 3

THEIR RIGHTS— AND YOURS

Iva Good had just left her office and was walking to her car when a man jumped her. The attacker yanked Iva's purse from her arm, ripped off her necklace, shoved her to the ground, and disappeared. Stunned, Iva felt helpless, powerless even to move. Her world seemed momentarily frozen. When she realized exactly what had happened and noted that her physical injuries were only scrapes and bruises, she gathered her strength and hurried back to her office to call the police.

After giving a description of the man to police officers, Iva worked with a police artist to create a composite picture. A short time later, after looking through mugshot books, she picked out a man named Rob Gan, recently paroled after serving three years of a ten-year sentence for assault. Officers found him in a nearby bar and began interrogating him.

From the time of the attack, however, Rob Gan was protected by a thick veil of legal rights. The United States Constitution has been interpreted by the highest courts as guaranteeing certain civil rights to all citizens. Over the course of many years, law has been developed on a case-by-case basis to ensure absolute fairness in the arrest and prosecution of every person. As a result, several rules of law must be followed by police in their investigation of crime. Courts, too, must meticulously follow these rights in the administration of justice. Individuals who are arrested have a right to an attorney; the right to remain silent; the right to question any searches of themselves, their homes, or their automobiles; the right to an arrest based on probable cause, and the right to be identified fairly. After arrest, every individual has the right to bail, the right to a trial by jury, the right to confront witnesses who testify against him or her, and many other defined rights, including the benefit of a reasonable doubt.

Victims' rights have been much slower to develop. Only in the last few years has there been a recognition by the criminal justice system that the victim too is entitled to fundamental human rights. No longer are only the Rob Gans protected by the system. Now the Iva Goods are guaranteed certain rights as well.

DEFENDANTS' RIGHTS

Police officers must be particularly careful in the course of an investigation. They must not infringe upon, but diligently protect, the rights of any suspect. Later the trial court will examine the officers' police work very carefully to ensure that all rights were protected. The trial court must uphold these rights. In turn, the trial court's work can be reviewed for fairness by an appeals court.

Statements and Confessions

Statements and confessions may be accepted in a court only if given voluntarily. As stated earlier, a suspect in a case must be advised of his constitutional rights to remain silent and to have an attorney. Every police officer, as part of his standard equipment, carries a "rights" card, which, at the appropriate time, is read to a suspect or defendant:

> *Before I ask you any questions you must understand your rights. You have the right to be silent. Anything you say can be used against you in court. You have the right to talk to a lawyer before I ask you any questions and have him with you during questioning. If you cannot pay for a lawyer one will be appointed for you by the court before any questioning if you wish. If you decide to answer questions now without a lawyer, you still have the right to stop answering questions at any time until you talk to a lawyer.*

Before any questioning occurs, the person being interrogated must indicate that he or she clearly understands these rights and still wishes to talk. If a police officer does not follow this procedure, any statements obtained or any information learned will not be admissible in any further proceeding against the person being questioned.

Sometimes higher courts change the rules after a case has been completed. A recent case in New York State prohibits a police officer from interrogating a suspect without his attorney present, even if he does not request an attorney, if the defendant has any other charges pending in which an attorney is representing him. This new ruling has disallowed the confessions of thousands of defendants who wanted to talk freely without their attorney present even though they had one in another pending case. The highest court in New York State made this rule retroactive, in effect changing the rules after the game was played. Cases many years old now must be held to the test of what is known as the "Rogers case." Decisions like this continue to be made, frequently altering the rights required in criminal law cases.

Search and Seizure

We are all protected against unreasonable searches of our homes, our cars, and our person. Searches conducted by police to obtain evidence may result in the arrest of the person who exercises control over (possesses) the property. To grant permission for a search, a judge issues a warrant. At times a search can be conducted without a warrant (such as when a police officer is within or on a property with the owner's permission). A police officer or a prosecutor can apply in writing for a search warrant, furnishing, under oath, information to the judge that there is probable cause to believe that certain items will be found in the area to be searched. This protection guarantees against unreasonable searches. Evidence seized without a search warrant is not admissible at trial.

Identifying the Defendant

A person charged has the right to be properly identified. The three methods of identification are a showup, a lineup, and a photo array.

If a victim confronts the person charged within moments of the violation, while the person is in police custody, the identification is known as a *showup*.

In a *lineup* several persons matching the same general description are lined up with the suspect. The victim is then asked to pick out the person who committed the act.

In a *photo array* identification, the victim selects one photo from among several photographs of different persons. All procedures must be conducted fairly, there can be no suggestion by the officer that any particular individual should be identified. Prior to trial, the defendant is entitled to a hearing to determine whether the identification was conducted fairly.

Other Rights Prior to Trial

A defendant is entitled to be certain that he or she has been arrested by a person having probable cause, that is, reasonable evidence that he or she committed the offense. The defendant is entitled to have bail set or to be released without bail.

Rights After the Arrest

After the arrest, many other defendants' rights come into play. Each person charged with a crime is entitled to legal counsel at the earliest stage of the proceeding. A defendant who requests an attorney must be provided with one without delay. If the defendant is unable to afford an attorney, the court must provide an attorney free of charge. In large communities staffs of public defenders or other attorneys who are sometimes called legal aid attorneys are available. In smaller communities, the judge appoints a private attorney.

Defendants are entitled to have bail set. In our legal system, a person who has been arrested is presumed innocent and should not be held in custody pending trial. You will learn how bail is set in Chapter 4.

Rights at a Trial

A person charged with a crime has the right, at the trial, to be confronted by his accuser and the right to cross-examine, through his attorney, witnesses who testify against him or her. In any criminal charge, a defendant is entitled to a trial by a jury, which must be held within a specific time after arrest.

Juries are comprised of people from a central pool of names obtained from either drivers' licenses or voter registration lists. Jurors sit as impartial judges of the facts and seek to determine the truth. Each person facing a criminal charge is presumed innocent until proved guilty. A defendant is not required to prove his or her innocence. The burden of proof is upon the prosecutor. Each and every element of a criminal charge must be proved beyond a reasonable doubt.

The presumption of innocence exists from the time a person is charged until the jurors or, if there is no jury, a judge, decides guilt or innocence. The defendant is found guilty only if the jury or judge is satisfied that the prosecutor has stripped away his presumption of innocence by proving the defendant guilty beyond a reasonable doubt. The defendant is entitled to a reasonable doubt. If a juror or the judge believes that there is a reason for doubting some required evidence that has been submitted to prove the defendant guilty, the judge or jury must find the defendant not guilty.

It follows that many prosecutors become frustrated when a defendant they know is guilty cannot be found legally guilty because they are unable to prove guilt beyond a reasonable doubt.

You should be aware that all defendants' rights ensure the integrity of the system; a defendant's rights can be met and still result in a successful prosecution. These rights exist not only for defendants but for you as ordinary citizens of our country. These rights have been given to us by the courts and the Constitution. They are changed and modified year by year, but, in general, they are intended to preserve all our freedoms for all time.

Defendants have a right to

- be protected from involuntary confessions or statements
- remain silent

- an attorney—if unable to afford one, to be provided with an attorney free of charge
- be free from unreasonable searches of property and person
- be fairly identified
- be arrested only when there is probable cause
- have bail set
- confront witnesses through cross-examination
- a jury trial
- a speedy trial

VICTIMS' RIGHTS

Whereas the rights of defendants are extensive, well established, and meticulously protected by the criminal justice system, the rights of victims are just beginning to be recognized. Advocacy and assistance programs have developed as the plight of victims has come to light and as the number of victims has reached astronomical heights. In the past decade the National Organization for Victim Assistance in Washington, D.C., among others, has served as both a clearinghouse and a legislative advocate in a campaign for victims' rights. Through its technical assistance and funding from government grants, victim and witness assistance programs have been established in communities throughout the country. Whether programs have been set up as a division of the local police department or the district attorney's office or as a private organization funded by government resources, they all serve to educate victims about their rights.

A person who becomes the victim of a crime frequently experiences a period of disorientation. The injuries, loss of belongings, and intrusion of privacy take their toll. Confusion and questions about what will happen next plague victims. Survivors of victims who have been killed experience anger and disbelief. This aftermath is a period marked by psychological trauma, fear, guilt, distrust, disbelief, and depression. Many victim-assistance groups specialize in helping victims through this difficult time and in putting their lives back together.

A victim has the right to know, and should demand to be kept up to date on, the status of his or her case. Because police and prosecutors are overwhelmed by the volume of their work, they often do not take the time to give victims progress reports.

If a suspect has been arrested, the victim is entitled to know whether the defendant was released on bail or remains in custody. The victim should alert the police of his or her fear of reprisal by a released defendant or by the defendant's family and request police protection.

Victims frequently have questions regarding what will face them in court, where the courtroom is located, waiting room facilities available, how much time is involved, the number of appearances in court before the case is actually called, and how to avoid a confrontation with the accused.

Streamlined procedures that eliminate unnecessary court appearances and waiting should be required, but this is often not the case. Victim-witness assistance programs are active in some areas. In California's Orange County the victim-assistance office is readily accessible as you walk into the courthouse. In some cases, if the victim is called to testify, a member of the victim-assistance group will accompany the victim to court, a particularly effective measure in eliminating a victim's uncertainty, fright, and fear of the court process. Compensation for out-of-pocket expenses, such as parking, babysitting, and lost work time, are not yet considered a right of victims, but advocates are working toward this goal.

Some states have passed legislation that requires less proof to prosecute certain cases. For example, in some areas the amount of proof required in sexual cases has been reduced. Many state laws require the prosecution in a rape case to show clear signs of injury to a nonsexual part of the victim's body. This requirement of *earnest resistance* is proof that the victim struggled to avoid the rape. However, this runs contrary to law enforcement directives that advise women not to struggle during a rape in order to avoid further serious injury or death. New York State law has removed this burden of proof for victims, although the prosecutor must still prove that the victim did not consent to sexual contact at the time of the attack. Now a threat of force or violence by the rapist is considered sufficient to show that the attack was committed without the victim's consent. Also, some states now prohibit testimony regarding the previous sexual activity of the rape victim.

Payment for Loss

Compensation for actual monetary losses should be paid by a defendant to his or her victim. Such compensation is often provided as part of a sentence or plea bargain arrangement. Sometimes, however, the loss is too great and/or the means of the defendant too few to provide adequate compensation. In most states, victim compensation boards provide compensation to victims of violent crimes for their injuries. Each year more states are added to the list and the amounts available are increased (see Appendix A).

A civil action filed against a person by his or her victim has always been an available remedy, though rarely used until recently. Now, many more persons who have been injured or suffered damages because of a burglar, rapist, or murderer are bringing civil lawsuits to obtain judgments in large amounts. Although the defendant may have no funds initially, future income can become the property of the victim. An inheritance, potential earnings, or other funds the defendant obtains may be used to satisfy a civil award to a victim. Some criminals write books about their experiences and realize royalties that can be legally diverted and seized after a civil judgment has been rendered enabling the victim to collect damages. Victims and their families have sued and collected damages from drunken drivers for years. Now victims of assaults, rapes, and other violent crimes are suing and winning, like the 15-year-old girl from Nebraska who was awarded a $22,500 judgment against the person who raped her. The lawsuit itself, which allows the victim the opportunity to make his or her feelings known to the defendant, often has a therapeutic value.

Third-party actions also have been recognized as avenues through which victims can seek compensation. In the state of Washington the prison warden who ran a "Take a Lifer to Dinner Program," under which inmates were allowed outside for brief periods, was sued after one of the dinner guests escaped and murdered a pawn-broker. The warden was held negligent because he did not have the authority to release the inmate even temporarily.

Recently, singer Connie Francis won a jury award of $2.5 million from Howard Johnson's Motels, Inc., after she was raped by a man who entered her room. She successfully argued that the motel room door locks, which could be opened with a little jiggling, were inadequate.

In another case in Washington, a 14-year-old school-girl was murdered by a psychiatric patient who was re-leased from a hospital without court approval. Her family brought legal action against the hospital and its officials, who were found negligent in releasing the patient. The staff, which had been informed that the patient was dan-gerous, had failed to follow recognized legal procedures. The court placed responsibility squarely on the hospital and its officials and later made a monetary award.

Currently, extending third-party liability to public of-ficials, such as a parole board that releases a potentially violent criminal early, is now being tested in the courts.

Other examples of third-party responsibility include landlords who provide inadequate security, hospitals who do not properly protect bedridden patients, and employers who improperly screen workers dealing in a sensitive public area (such as a landlord who gives a passkey to a worker who may have a record).

Victims have a right to

- be free from fear of reprisal
- be free from fear of the unknown in court
- be informed when an arrest is made and whether the defendant is in custody
- be kept informed of case progress and be permitted to give input
- be called to testify in court only when necessary
- be paid in full for monetary losses
- file a civil action against the person who has committed the wrong
- sue third parties who contribute to a defendant's improper conduct

Victims' rights continue to evolve. Victims who have acted successfully to protect their rights are described in the case section of this book.

CHAPTER 4
THE FELONY

DISCOVERY TO SENTENCE

Bill and Pat Conner had just spent a fine evening in the city—dinner and the theater. Returning to their fashionable suburban home, they noticed that the outdoor lights they thought they had turned on earlier, were out. After parking the car in the garage, Bill put his key in the door that led from the garage into the kitchen. The door swung open without a turn of the key. As he switched on a light he saw a man in his mid-twenties carrying a pillowcase, filled with goods. Bill rushed back into the garage where Pat had waited, grabbed her arm, and ran with her to a neighbor's house to call the police. He reported a burglary in progress and gave a description of the intruder.

Lights out that you thought you had left on, open doors, and broken windows all are signs of an intrusion. Don't

be brave. Don't try to investigate. If you sense that somebody is in your house, that a break-in has occurred, keep
cool, use your head, and do not force a confrontation.
Go immediately to the nearest telephone and call the
police. Many areas have a 911 emergency number; others
have the full seven-digit code. There are inevitably situations where you may need to call the police from your
home, so be prepared and have emergency numbers
nearby. Phone stickers for the types of numbers you need
in a hurry are often available from local authorities. You
can also always call the telephone operator. This takes a
little longer than the direct numbers, but you will be put
through as fast as the operator can manage. When you
contact the police, give your name, the trouble you wish
to report (preferably in less than ten words), and the
address. Answer questions asked by the police operator
concisely. Follow directions.

When you discover a crime being committed

- go to a safe place
- do not interrupt or confront the intruder
- remember the description, including face, clothing,
  size, and any unusual features or characteristics
- contact the police
- be brief and precise with the police operator

When the Police Arrive

*Within minutes several police patrol cars reached the
vicinity of the Conner home. Several blocks away, a*

police officer spotted a person matching the description Bill had given. Within a few more minutes, police technicians arrived at the Conner house and set about taking photographs, dusting for fingerprints, and performing other technical functions. Four other police officers roamed through the house examining each room, looking for clues. They noticed that dresser drawers, dining room drawers, and cabinets had been opened and ransacked. Bill and Pat were asked very specific questions. "When did you leave? Did you lock the doors? Were the lights left on? Have you been burglarized before? Where do you keep your valuables? Do you know what is missing?"

An early assessment revealed that the gold railroad watch of Pat's grandfather, a television set, and many pieces of sterling silver, including Bill's initialed sterling silver college drinking cup, were missing. In the porch entrance technicians found a piece of a television antenna.

Sergeant Bill Goldman, who was in charge of the investigation, assured the Conners that the police would do everything possible to catch the burglar. He told them that there had been many break-ins in the neighborhood recently. He also asked the Conners to compile a list of missing items. At 3 A.M. the police left. Bill and Pat, understandably, were upset and couldn't sleep; knowing that a stranger had invaded the privacy of their home and taken their possessions rattled them thoroughly.

Always cooperate with the police. One officer will be in charge of your investigation, and he is the person to whom you should give all the information required. Do not enter the crime scene or disturb anything until the police indicate you may do so. The crime scene must be left undisturbed so that fingerprints and photographs may be taken, if required.

You will be asked many questions when a criminal report is taken, and the report will include information about you. Although it may seem unimportant to you, little bits and pieces of information concerning your case help police officers determine and identify patterns of the same types of crime. A burglar known to police may have a certain method of operation. Do not do your own police work.

When the police arrive

- learn the identity of the officer in charge of the investigation
- answer concisely all questions asked by the police
- provide a description of any suspects
- provide a list of damage or missing goods
- do not enter crime scene until you obtain police approval

Police Identification

The next morning Bill was asked to go to the police station to look at some photographs. Detective Ed O'Grodnik showed him an array of seven photographs, commonly called mug shots, of young men with features similar to those in the description Bill had given. Bill identified the intruder by the horizontal two-inch scar on his left cheek. The person in the photo was John Rowe, 25, who had been in trouble in the past for shoplifting and other petty thievery.

O'Grodnik told Bill that Rowe had been stopped on the street near his home after a foot chase by two officers. Rowe had been placed in a patrol vehicle, searched, and advised of his constitutional rights. The gold watch of Pat's grandfather was found in Rowe's pocket. This evidence, together with Bill's positive identification, provided the probable cause for an arrest. But the detective told Bill that a second person must have been involved because of the number of items taken. O'Grodnik also reported that Rowe refused to talk.

Identification by a victim or witness is essential when a suspect is charged with a crime. The law requires that this procedure be done fairly. The detective correctly showed Bill several similar photos so as not to suggest to him which one was the culprit.

An in-person lineup, another form of identification, is not always practical; it is time consuming and may be difficult because of the need to quickly obtain people with similar features. Photographic identification, which is easy to conduct, is also less intimidating to the victim.

The third form of identification, the informal showup, occurs when a suspect has been detained by the police within moments after a crime has been reported. The identification may take place at the scene of the crime, in a police station, or in a police car.

The Arrest

Shortly after the foot chase, John Rowe was taken to police headquarters. A felony complaint charged John Rowe with burglary and grand larceny.

A person is arrested when the police, having probable cause to believe he or she has committed a crime, exercise physical control over him or her. The specific charge made against a person is determined *after* the facts are reviewed and applied to elements of a crime in the state penal law. The document bearing the charge in this case is the felony complaint. It is filed in the court that has jurisdiction over the area in which the crime was committed.

Arraignment: The First Court Appearance

John Rowe was held in a police lockup until the next morning, at which time he was arraigned in City Court, the local criminal court. At such time, all persons arrested in the city since the previous day or the last session of court, are arraigned, meaning that the court obtains jurisdiction or control over the defendant.

Rowe was one of thirty-five persons arrested during the past 24 hours. They included a couple of shoplifters, two prostitutes, a person held for a family offense, and two burglars. One person had been arrested for serious assault and many others for disorderly conduct and trespass. John Rowe was one of the burglars.

At 9:30 A.M., as Judge Roy Davis walked into the courtroom, the bailiff said, "All rise. City Court is now in session." The judge sat high on the bench with a lot of paperwork in front of him. Facing the bench were a public defender and his staff, ready to represent anyone who could not afford a lawyer. Seated at a nearby table was a member of the pretrial release organization, ready to make recommendations on release of the person in custody. The assistant district attorney stood at the podium. Between the people and the judge sat the court reporter who was writing down everything official said in court. Two court clerks kept track of all paperwork. A court attendant and two policemen were present to assist in keeping order in the court and to transport prisoners. A policewoman stood guard over the two women arrested on prostitution charges.

John Rowe's name was announced. Rowe was directed to the microphone next to the district attorney. The judge read from the felony complaint, "John Rowe, you are charged with burglary in the second degree, having unlawfully entered and remained in a house last night with the intent of committing a crime of larceny. Do you have a lawyer?" Rowe said he couldn't afford a lawyer, that he wasn't working and had no assets.

Bill Brongo, the assistant public defender, stood up and said he would represent Rowe. It was now time to consider the plea. After a few private words with the defendant, Brongo said, "Your Honor, John Rowe enters a plea of not guilty, and I reserve all of his rights." Judge Davis replied, "Very well, a plea of not guilty is entered."

The judge turned to the district attorney and asked if he had a bail recommendation.

"Yes, your Honor. This was a house burglary. There have been a lot of them in the area recently. I am recommending bail in the amount of $5,000."

The judge turned to Bill White at the pretrial release table. White said Rowe qualified for release. Although Rowe was not living at home, he could return to live with his mother, who would assure his appearance in court. The judge reviewed Rowe's prior record, which included five arrests in the past eighteen months, all for different forms of theft. If eventually convicted on this charge, Rowe would be facing a long jail sentence. Therefore, the judge should have some security to assure the defendant's appearance. Bail was set in the amount of $2,000 as a secured bond. Judge Davis granted the public defender's request for a preliminary hearing within 72 hours to determine if the defendant should continue to be held for trial. John Rowe was held in custody pending the hearing.

The arraignment is the formal exercise of the court's power and control over a defendant. At the arraignment the defendant must answer the charge with a plea of guilty or not guilty. If a plea of guilty is entered after the person has been advised of all his rights, including the right to trial, a sentence can be imposed. In felony cases, however, even if the defendant has given a full confession, a plea of guilty cannot be entered at the initial arraignment. Local criminal courts do not have the power to accept guilty pleas in felony cases. The entry of a not guilty plea is a formality in felonies. It merely gives the court power to set bail and release the defendant pending further proceedings or hold him for the preliminary hearing so that his case can be referred to the Superior Court, the trial court for felonies.

At the arraignment

- the local court exercises power and control over the defendant
- a lawyer appears with the defendant or is assigned to the defendant
- a plea of not guilty is entered
- the defendant's release on bail or other grounds is considered
- a preliminary hearing may be scheduled

Bail

Bail, which is determined at the arraignment, is used to secure a defendant's appearance at subsequent court hearings. It is not used to punish a defendant for a crime of which he or she has not yet been convicted.

A judge considers various factors in setting bail, including the prior record of the defendant, his or her ties to the local community, and the individual's family situation. Bail is usually higher in the more serious cases, particularly those with a mandatory jail sentence. The likelihood of a person's returning to court is the bottom-line consideration in determining the amount of bail. Bail may be either cash or a secured bond placed by a bail bondsman, who is paid a cash premium, usually equal to 10 percent of the bond. He then guarantees to the court that if the defendant does not appear he will pay the full amount of the bail. Consequently, bail bondsmen, who are licensed by the state, have a financial interest in seeing that defendants return to court.

In some areas, a personal recognizance bond, which is an unsecured bond, is allowed. When a person charged subsequently does not appear in court, he, or a person vouching for him, faces a civil judgment for the amount of the bail.

Bail conditions are determined by

- the probability of the defendant's returning to court
- the age, occupation, and family situation of the defendant
- the impact on the community of the release of the defendant

A person may be released without posting bail. A typical case is a young person without a prior criminal record living with his parents who will guarantee his court appearances.

A third type of release is a pretrial release, where bail is unnecessary. In many communities pretrial-release organizations interview defendants and make recommendations to the judge based upon a point scoring system, which measures the likelihood of a defendant's returning to court. Pretrial-release organizations monitor each in-

dividual's release and send reminders of court appearance
dates to defendants.

The Preliminary Hearing

*Detective O'Grodnik called Bill to request his presence
in court to testify at the preliminary hearing. Now Bill
would have his first face-to-face confrontation with the
defendant since walking into the house three nights earlier. He would have to identify Rowe in court and the
gold watch that had been given to Pat by her grandfather.
Bill was told to be at court early to meet the district
attorney and prepare for court.*

*Bill found Judge Davis' courtroom, where he met
O'Grodnik. They went into an adjacent office where Bill
was introduced to Assistant District Attorney Sheldon
Boyce. Boyce told Bill that a preliminary hearing was
not the trial but only a short hearing to determine if there
was reasonable cause to believe the defendant had committed the crime. Boyce outlined what he had learned
about the case. He said he would ask Bill to identify the
gold watch and point out the defendant in the courtroom.
The officer who had stopped Rowe on the street would
also be in court to tell the judge about the arrest. No
jury would be present. If the judge found that there was
reasonable cause to believe the defendant had committed
the crime, he would order him held in custody and refer
his case to the grand jury in the Superior Criminal Court.*

*An hour later, the case was called. Rowe, flanked by
two police officers, entered the courtroom. The first wit-*

ness was Officer Dick Lambrix, who told about arresting Rowe. The officer was cross-examined in detail by Public Defender Brongo. Bill was not permitted to hear the officer's testimony. Often the judge permits a witness in the courtroom only when it is his or her time to testify. In this way one witness's testimony will not influence what another witness will say. This policy assures an independent recollection of the facts.

Bill was called to testify and directed to the witness stand next to the judge. He raised his right hand, taking an oath to tell the truth. The district attorney asked questions about the watch and then asked Bill to look around the courtroom to determine if he could identify the person he saw going through his house. Bill recognized the person with the two-inch scar. Pointing to Rowe, he said, "Yes, that's the man." Bill was rigorously cross-examined for a half hour by the public defender.

In a preliminary hearing, the defense usually presents no witnesses, and instead waits until the actual trial in Superior Court. This case was no exception. After the district attorney was finished presenting evidence, the defense attorney announced there would be no defense witnesses. He asked that the case be dismissed for failure to present sufficient proof. Judge Davis denied the motion, saying there was enough evidence to hold the defendant for action in the Superior Court. The judge continued bail at $2,000 secured bond, which Rowe could not raise.

Bill Conner was free to go. As he left the courtroom, the assistant district attorney told him that he might be called again to testify in a few weeks before the grand jury.

A preliminary hearing in a felony

- is usually held within 72 hours of arraignment
- is held to determine if there is reasonable cause to believe the defendant committed the crime
- is before a judge only
- is the first formal court confrontation with the defendant
- determines whether the case should be sent to the grand jury

The Grand Jury

The grand jury, which is selected by the commissioner of jurors, includes from sixteen to twenty-three citizens from the community. Impaneled by the Superior Court for a period of up to a month, the grand jury hears several cases a day involving felony accusations. It hears the evidence, just as Judge Davis did, and decides whether the evidence is sufficient to warrant a trial in Superior Court.

Bill was asked to testify before the grand jury. The only persons allowed in the grand jury room are the district attorney, the court reporter, witnesses, and, of course, the grand jurors. Neither the judge, defendant, nor defense attorney is present. After listening to the testimony, the grand jury decides by majority vote whether to issue an indictment, or a *true bill*. This is a felony accusation that must be answered in the Superior Court, where all further proceedings are held.

When the grand jury finds the evidence insufficient to continue to charge the defendant, a *no bill* is rendered. The charge is dismissed and if the defendant is in custody, he or she will be released.

Sometimes, as an alternative, the grand jury directs the district attorney to file a misdemeanor or petty offense infraction as a new charge in a local criminal court for prosecution.

In a few states, including California, the grand jury is limited to investigations of misconduct by public officials. Other cases are referred to the Superior Court based upon the decision of the district attorney.

In all states it has become standard practice to dispense with a preliminary hearing when a defendant is released from custody after arraignment. Instead, the matter may go either directly to the Superior Court or to the grand jury, which decides whether the charge will be heard in Superior Court.

A grand jury

- is composed of sixteen to twenty-three community members
- hears the evidence in felony accusations; neither the judge, the defendant, nor the defense attorney is present
- files an indictment, or true bill, in Superior Court

when a majority of the grand jury agrees that a
charge should be made
- files a "no bill" when no charge is made
- is not always used; in some states the decision to
refer a case to Superior Court is made by the district
attorney

Arraignment After
Grand Jury Indictment

*When the grand jury handed down a unanimous decision,
the case of John Rowe was referred to Superior Court,
the trial level for felony cases, where all future proceedings of his case will be held. (If the defendant is being
held in custody, the arraignment is held on the first court
date after the grand jury proceeding; if the defendant is
not in custody, however, the arraignment usually takes
place within a week of the grand jury proceeding. Or,
the judge may order that the defendant be picked up
immediately.)*

Judge Culver of the Superior Court called the case,
People of the State of New York *v.* John Rowe. *The
district attorney read the indictment, which charged John
Rowe with burglary and grand larceny.*

*Public Defender Brongo once again entered a plea of
not guilty for Rowe. He asked that Rowe be released
because he had been held in custody for two weeks and
could not make the $2,000 bond. Again, the pretrial
representative recommended to the judge that on points
Rowe could be released to his mother. The judge required*

the bond. The judge then notified the attorneys that they had two weeks to disclose their files to each other, following which the case would be scheduled for motions on the court calendar.

Pretrial Procedures

During the following two weeks all reports, statements (none in this case), details of photo identification, and other information were exchanged by the attorneys.

Criminal law is not the cloak-and-dagger courtroom event you may think it to be. Rarely is there a surprise. Well in advance of trial, each side furnishes the other with a theory of its case, the names of witnesses who may testify, scientific reports, and anything else that will be used in the case. This is done informally at times and at other times on order of a judge based on an attorney's request.

Many find this open file approach surprising. It is done to allow each side to evaluate its position in relation to that of its opponent, which tends to encourage a fair and final disposition of a case without the necessity of going to trial. More than 95 percent of all criminal cases do not actually have full trials. They are either dismissed, a lesser plea is agreed upon, or the defendant pleads guilty as charged.

Before trial a defense attorney knows whether a statement or confession was given to the police by the defendant and whether a search by the police and a pretrial identification procedure were conducted. The defense attorney can then determine if he should ask for one or

more hearings before the judge to determine if these procedures were conducted in accordance with the constitutional rights of the defendant. If hearings are requested,
they are held before the trial judge prior to the actual
trial.

If the judge determines that the statement was given
involuntarily and that the constitutional rights of the defendant were not met, he or she will suppress the statement, that is, prohibit it from being offered as evidence.
If he or she finds a search invalid, anything obtained
from the search will not be admissible as evidence at the
trial. If a lineup was conducted unfairly, it, too, will be
suppressed.

All these factors are considered in evaluating the relevant strengths and weaknesses of both the case for the
prosecution and for the defense.

In pretrial procedures

- each side discloses to the other the facts it knows
  about the case
- hearings are sometimes scheduled to determine the
  admissibility of confessions; whether the proper legal steps were taken in seizing evidence; and whether
  the defendant's rights were protected during the
  identification procedure

Plea Bargaining

*If convicted on the burglary charge, John Rowe faces a
sentence of up to ten years in a state prison.*

Depending on his case backlog and the strength of the individual case, the district attorney may decide to offer the defendant a reduced charge to a lesser degree felony that requires a maximum sentence of only four years in state prison. In making this decision he considers the area where the crime occurred, the input of the police, and any special circumstances affecting the defendant. The feelings of the victim, the restitution required, and how the victim presents himself or herself as a witness are also important considerations.

Plea bargaining is a valuable procedure within the court process. It is a time for both attorneys to evaluate the quality of their cases. The district attorney, realizing that he must convince a jury beyond a reasonable doubt of his position, may discover some weaknesses. The defense attorney will try to lessen the severity of the crime if he believes the probability of conviction is high. Both sides attain certainty and remove the risks.

Plea bargaining reduces a potentially staggering case backlog that would exist but for the small percentage of cases that actually go to trial. The result is that resolutions in those cases are reached speedily. Much plea bargaining is done in the presence of the judge, with full disclosure on the court record. Plea bargaining also spares witnesses and victims an uncertain result and eliminates their need to testify and come to court.

Another option is sentence bargaining. If a mandatory sentence is not required by state law, the defendant may exchange a plea of guilty for a sentence of either probation or a shorter jail term. Many factors are considered in sentence bargaining, including the attitude of the defendant, chances for rehabilitation, circumstances of the arrest, and the strength of the case from the point of view of both the defense and the prosecution.

Brongo discussed the case in full with John Rowe. He explained to Rowe that after reviewing all the facts it appeared that the prosecutor would have an easy job convicting him. Not only had he been found with evidence in his pocket, but the victim could positively identify him. Brongo had learned these facts at the preliminary hearing. Rowe told Brongo that he would like to reveal to the district attorney the name of his accomplice in exchange for a lesser plea or a reduced sentence.

Sometimes the district attorney will grant immunity from prosecution or offer a plea to a lesser charge if the defendant agrees to testify against another person whom the people want to convict. In this case, the district attorney was told that the person to be identified was implicated in dozens of other burglaries and that Rowe would talk about the burglaries and point out to the police the houses where they had done other jobs. The police could close their investigations on other break-ins, let the victims know that the intruders had been apprehended, and perhaps convict the accomplice, who was more active in burglary operations, on a more severe charge for a longer sentence.

John Rowe would have to testify at his co-conspirator's trial. He would also have to disclose that he would receive a lesser sentence in return for his testimony. The district attorney accepted Rowe's offer.

In the company of his attorney, Rowe told a long tale of the many burglaries he had committed with Sam Sturg, a previously convicted felon. If convicted a second time on a felony charge, Sturg would receive a mandatory maximum sentence of twenty years. Based upon the information the police had now put together, Assistant District Attorney Boyce, working with Detective O'Grodnik, applied to Judge Culver for a search warrant for Sturg's home. Police used the search warrant the next day while Sam was in the house watching a program on Bill Conner's television set. The police recognized Bill's television set from the original identification and also matched the antenna part that had been knocked off in the burglary.

Nearly two months after the break-in at his house, Bill was called back to the police department to positively identify the television set. He was also told that he might be needed to testify at Sam Sturg's trial, where he would have to describe the burglary and identify his television set.

Plea bargaining

- reduces case backlog
- takes into consideration the strengths and the weaknesses of each side's case
- attempts to achieve an early conclusion of the case
- should consider the victim's feelings
- results in a plea of guilty to a lesser charge and a consequent shorter maximum sentence

The Felony Trial

Sam Sturg was arrested but could not make his $10,000 bail. He, too, had a preliminary hearing.

The twelve-member jury for his trial was selected by the attorneys in front of the judge, a process called the *voir dire*. Literally translated, the phrase means "to look and say," that is, to examine prospective jurors to determine whether or not they will be fair. Both defense and prosecution attorneys are interested in finding jurors with open minds who will be able to set aside any personal prejudices or experiences to reach a fair decision. Jurors must determine the truth of the facts presented.

The judge's function in a jury trial is to interpret the law and rule on motions. At the conclusion of the case the judge instructs the jury members on the law and the specific elements they must apply to render a verdict of guilty or not guilty. The jury's verdict must be unanimous. If the verdict is not unanimous, the jury is termed a "hung jury." The case must then be retried before a new jury.

In felony jury trials

- a jury of twelve persons is selected by attorneys in the presence of a judge
- the judge explains the law
- the jury determines the truth of all the facts
- the case will be retried when the verdict is not unanimous

At the trial the judge makes an opening statement to the jury, explaining certain items of law, including the defendant's presumed innocence, the burden of proof on the prosecution, and the importance of the credibility of the evidence. Then the district attorney makes an opening

statement, which outlines all the points he will attempt
to prove. Next, the defense attorney makes an opening
statement, but only if he or she chooses to do so. After
the opening statements, the district attorney calls his first
witness. Every individual called to testify does so under
oath and each is subject to cross-examination by the defense attorney.

*In Sam Sturg's case the district attorney called a parade
of witnesses, beginning with Sergeant Bill Goldman, the
officer in charge of the investigation at Bill and Pat
Conner's house. The district attorney also called Pat, to
identify her grandfather's watch, and Bill, to identify the
TV set and describe the scene of the crime. Both Pat and
Bill were asked to identify photographs of the crime scene.
Stan Avery, a fingerprint expert who had found Sam's
print on a tray, and other evidence technicians were
called. Sergeant O'Grodnik testified about finding the
television set while Sam was watching it. John Rowe was
the district attorney's final, as well as his star, witness.
Roy Lockwood, Sturg's attorney, questioned all of the
witnesses at great length. After all the prosecution witnesses have testified, the district attorney announces to
the courtroom, "Let the people rest," which means that
he has completed the presentation of all direct evidence.*
*The defendant now has an opportunity to testify or
present proof of innocence on his own behalf. At Sturg's
request, Roy Lockwood called several of Sturg's old
friends to testify that he was playing pool on the night
of the burglary. Cross-examination revealed that none of
Sturg's friends could specifically say that he was actually*

at the pool hall for the entire evening. Knee High Stone, in fact, revealed that Sturg had left the pool hall for a couple of hours that evening.

Sturg did not testify. No defendant is required to testify in his own defense, nor can juries infer any guilt because a defendant remains silent.

Testimony in the case was now complete. The next stage in the trial is known as "closing the proof." Lockwood made his closing remarks or summation. Next, the district attorney summed up his view of the facts.

In every criminal trial, the prosecutor begins the trial with an opening statement and concludes it with his closing remarks. Although the prosecutor has the burden of proof, his right to open and close the trial is believed to be an advantage.

The judge spent several minutes giving the charge to the jury. He emphasized that the burden of proof rests with the prosecutor, and that the defendant is presumed innocent until proved guilty. He carefully defined reasonable doubt and detailed the elements of the crime of burglary. The jury members were told to apply the facts they believed to be true to the law as explained by the judge and come out with a verdict. The judge outlined their options regarding a verdict. The jury was admonished not to be concerned with any possible sentence or punishment that could be imposed. Sentencing and punishment are the province of the judge.

In the case of the People v. Sam Sturg, *the jury deliberated behind closed doors for two hours. After notifying the court attendant that a verdict had been reached, the jury filed back into the courtroom. The foreman, the person selected to be the spokesperson for the jury, announced the verdict: guilty.*

The order of procedure of a jury trial includes

- jury selection
- judge's opening statement
- prosecutor's opening statement
- defense attorney's opening statement if desired
- prosecution's case, which must prove all the elements of the crime as charged beyond a reasonable doubt
- defense's case
- summation of defense
- summation of prosecution
- charge to the jury by the judge
- deliberation of the jury and the return of a verdict by the jury

POST-CONVICTION PROCEDURE

After the verdict, the judge adjourns the case for two weeks to allow the county probation department to prepare a pre-sentencing report. The report contains a statement of the crime; a history of the defendant's background, including criminal activity; any aptitude or testing information; family data; and a recommendation by the probation department regarding sentencing. The judge may also receive a report from the defense attorney and any members of the community who wish to communicate with him regarding the case.

On the day of sentencing, Sturg was returned to court and sentenced to up to twenty years in the state prison. In exchange for his cooperation, John Rowe was sentenced to two to four years, making him eligible for parole in sixteen months.

In determining a sentence, a judge must follow the requirements of the law. At times mandatory jail sentences, particularly with repeat felony offenders, are required. Other jail sentences may be optional and imposed if appropriate.

Probation is often another option. Probation is a period of time, several years in duration, during which a defendant must report regularly to a probation officer. The defendant must live up to certain conditions outlined by the judge or probation officer. Regular employment, staying out of trouble, counseling, and making restitution are possible conditions of probation. When a person violates the terms of probation, a brief hearing is held. The individual can be resentenced by the judge in accordance with the original sentencing options, which might include jail.

In the cases *People* v. *John Rowe* and *People* v. *Sam Sturg* many factors were noted to familiarize you with the orderly flow of procedure in a felony case. Whenever an arrest is followed by full prosecution, variables can occur. Not all cases are as neat and as well prosecuted as the two presented here. The victims were helpful and willing to testify. They gave up a lot of time without being compensated by the court. Whether Bill and Pat will ever be repaid is unknown. How much they will ultimately recover from the invasion of their privacy is another unknown. To prevent future break-ins, the Conners have installed a $2,000 burglar alarm system, which is no guarantee, of course, that another break-in won't occur. They hope, however, that this expenditure will give them peace of mind—and perhaps prevent a similar occurrence—and ordeal.

APPEALS

Appeals are commonly pursued in convictions that result in a jail sentence. No new testimony is taken at the Appeals Court level and victims do not appear. The judges who decide the appeal read the transcript of the trial and listen to oral arguments by the district attorney and the defense attorney. If a mistake was made that substantially affected the rights of the defendant, the conviction may be overturned and the case retried. Further, if the Appeals Court believes that the jury or judge did not properly follow the evidence, the conviction may be overturned and the case dismissed. Although appeals are frequent, reversals are rare.

CHAPTER 5

PROSECUTIONS FOR MISDEMEANORS AND PETTY OFFENSE INFRACTIONS

Awakened abruptly by the sound of a car racing near his home, Loren Kroll jumped out of bed, looked out the window, and saw a late-model sports car swerve across his lawn, knock over the mailbox, and disappear into the night.

In those few seconds, he committed the first few numbers of the license plate to memory, got a general description of the automobile, and noted that there were two occupants.

Loren was understandably upset, particularly so because he had just purchased the mailbox and had spent much of the previous day painting and lettering it. He immediately called the police, gave his name and address, told the police operator what had just happened, and also provided a description and direction of travel of the vehicle.

REPORTING THE INCIDENT

You must observe as many details of an incident as possible to assist the police in apprehending the person responsible for the damage. Always have the phone number of your local police handy to save precious seconds. As noted earlier, briefly state your name and the address of the incident, explain what occurred in just a few words, and answer the questions of the police operator directly. In this type of case, remember that your observations are important because investigation time will be limited. Police priority is given to more important felonies.

In reporting the incident

- make detailed observations
- have the phone number of the local police posted near your phone
- call the police at once
- give your name, address, and a concise statement of what occurred; answer the questions of the police operator
- wait for the police officer to arrive

Officer Mike Belle-Isle arrived within moments. Together with Loren, he observed skid marks on the lawn near the demolished mailbox. Within minutes another police officer stopped a car matching Loren's original description. The car had mud on its tires and a small dent on the right front fender. The fresh paint scratches on the fender appeared to match the paint on Loren's mailbox.

Kevin Boyle, the sports car driver, admitted he had made a wide racing turn while showing off to his girlfriend, Mary Beth. The second officer directed Boyle to drive the car back to the accident scene, where Loren positively identified it.

THE ARREST

Officer Belle-Isle outlined the criminal charge that could be filed because of Boyle's admission, the physical evidence, and Loren's observations. The victim agreed with the police officer's advice that the driver be arrested for the misdemeanor, or criminal mischief. Loren was asked to fill out the necessary papers, outlining the facts exactly as he observed them. Officer Belle-Isle told Loren to obtain a written estimate of the damages and directed Boyle to drive his car to the police station.

In this case, a police technician was not called nor were photographs taken. The defendant admitted his act. The observations made by the police officers were sufficient to eliminate the need for fingerprints and photographs. A result could be achieved in this case without high-priced police work.

Although far more numerous than felonies, crimes and offenses of less significance are often treated routinely— without much personal attention. If results are to be achieved through the use of the courts, the victim must take the initiative.

The decision to file a charge in misdemeanor cases is

often left to the victim. The police officer informs the victim of the procedure to follow in placing a charge. In many locales the police make the actual arrest and file the arrest document. The victim only fills out a supporting deposition, which consists of giving a written statement of the facts under oath. This is often true when the incident has just happened and the police investigation results in a quick arrest.

In some situations, the victim is required to make the complaint and fill out the accusatory instrument, which forms the sole basis of the charge. To do this, the victim signs all documents while under oath. A misdemeanor is still prosecuted in the name of the People of the State.

In a misdemeanor arrest

- the police instruct you on the procedure to follow
- the police officer, at your request, files charges after making an investigation
- you may be required to file a supporting deposition
- you may sometimes be required to file the actual accusatory instrument on your own initiative
- the defendant is prosecuted in the name of the People of the State

By now Loren had gone back to sleep. Boyle was in the police station with Officer Belle-Isle, who was filling out the necessary arrest papers. He released Boyle and told him to be in court the following Monday. As a reminder to come to court, the officer gave Boyle an appearance ticket, much like a traffic ticket, but did not require him to post bail.

Unlike felony cases, misdemeanors, or petty offense violations, do not require the arraignment of the defendant before he is released from custody. An appearance ticket is often given, directing him to appear in court for arraignment. The police officer, who determines whether the defendant is likely to return to court, considers the defendant's age, job, and family and community ties; the nature of the charge; and any prior criminal record. When a defendant does not show up in accordance with the appearance ticket, the court directs that a warrant of arrest be issued. A police officer then brings the defendant to court.

Police also can require bail to be posted at the police station in misdemeanor, or petty offense, cases. Bail is then forwarded to the court.

In misdemeanor cases

- an appearance ticket is issued to the defendant after processing
- bail is sometimes required, but it can be posted at the police department
- the defendant can be held in custody for arraignment before a judge

In addition to the nature of the charge, release of a defendant in misdemeanor cases is based on the defendant's

- family ties in the community
- place of work
- family situation
- prior criminal record

Sometimes the police officer detains the defendant in misdemeanor or petty offense cases, until a judge can make a bail decision. This is true in cases of violent acts when it is wise to deny access of the defendant to the victim for a period of time. When there has been a fight or family dispute and there is a potential for injury, a cooling-off period may be necessary.

The driver of the sports car appeared in court at the appointed time. Judge Davis, who had presided in the case of the burglars, Rowe and Sturg, was again presiding.

The judge explained the charges to Boyle and told him that a misdemeanor conviction could result in a criminal record. He told Boyle he should have an attorney. A "not guilty" plea was entered, reserving Boyle's rights until an attorney could appear with him. Throughout the arraignment, the court had exercised its power of jurisdiction over Boyle. Judge Davis continued Boyle's release on his own recognizance until the next court date.

Within a couple of days Loren Kroll delivered to Officer Belle-Isle estimates totaling $125 to repair his lawn and mailbox. Belle-Isle passed the information on to the district attorney.

To follow through in misdemeanor cases a victim must

- obtain written estimates of the damage
- notify the police or district attorney in writing of the damage estimates

On the next court date, Kevin Boyle appeared with his attorney, Steve Philip. Philip had evaluated the case, which was to be heard in the local criminal court because it was a misdemeanor. His client was entitled to a hearing to determine whether his confession was obtained properly. He was also entitled to a jury trial of six people, one-half the number of jurors in a felony trial. Because of his client's clean record and his willingness to pay Kroll the amount of $125, Philip engaged in plea bargaining with Assistant District Attorney Sheldon Boyce in an effort to protect his client from a criminal record. Boyce knew he had a good case; however, he talked to Loren Kroll and learned that he was mainly concerned with preventing Boyle from repeating the act and being paid the $125 for damages. Boyce offered the defendant a plea to the petty offense violation of disorderly conduct, a non-crime, if he agreed to pay $125 directly to Loren. Philip thought the bargain a good solution and advised Boyle to enter the plea.

Few misdemeanor cases ever go to trial. Many are withdrawn by the people who file the charges. A high percentage are withdrawn or dismissed because the victim does not appear. Others are treated routinely, often in a disinterested way, by court personnel because the victim has failed to follow through in supplying necessary information to the district attorney or the court. When the district attorney does have sufficient information, plea bargaining frequently occurs. The large number of these cases prohibits extended trials.

The district attorney is primarily concerned with

achieving the best possible result. In the case described
above, the victim would be paid promptly. He would not
have to go to court and be further inconvenienced but
would obtain the desired results through the defendant's
plea to a lesser charge.

Misdemeanors and petty offenses are

- routinely dismissed if the victim does not cooperate
- dismissed if the victim does not appear in court
  when summoned
- often resolved through plea bargaining
- tried by a judge or in some cases a six-person jury

*Both Boyle's lawyer and the assistant district attorney
consulted with Judge Davis, who agreed to the lesser
charge. The judge asked Boyle what his plea was to the
new and reduced charge of disorderly conduct. Boyle
said, "Guilty." The judge asked him what he had done.
Boyle related the story and said he was sorry for his
actions. The judge noted that Boyle had no prior record
and expressed his belief that the incident had resulted
from carelessness rather than any intent to harm. The
judge ordered Boyle to pay the victim $125. Boyle was
given one week to produce a bank draft payable to Loren
Kroll. If he had not been able to pay it that quickly, the
judge would have set up a payment schedule. If any
payments were missed, he would be called back into court
and could be resentenced. The judge briefly lectured Boyle
and told him that a similar incident within the next year*

would result in resentencing, possibly either a large fine or a jail sentence. This is called conditional discharge.

In misdemeanor cases, the judge has many options in sentencing. Depending on the class of misdemeanor, a jail sentence of up to one year can be imposed. Often when defendants are employed, weekend sentences are used as an alternative. Other options include fines up to $1,000, probation supervised by a probation officer, and conditional discharge. In some communities, innovative judges have required defendants to work directly for their victims for an assigned number of hours. Another alternative is community service sentencing, which requires a defendant to work a prescribed number of hours on public projects, such as assisting senior citizens.

Misdemeanor sentences include

- jail for up to one year
- weekend sentences
- fines up to $1,000
- probation
- community work projects
- conditional discharge

OTHER ALTERNATIVES

Mary Moran, an office worker, had just come home and was relaxing before dinner. For the fourth time in three

*days, her former boyfriend, Larry Blue, called to tell her
he couldn't live without her. Although she firmly told him
not to call her again, the telephone rang several times
during the next few nights. Finally she answered it, only
to hear Blue say, "If you go out with another man, I'll
make your face look like it went through a meat grinder."*

*Frightened, Mary called the police. The operator told
her that he would take a report over the phone, but that
if she wanted to have Blue arrested, she would have to
file a complaint for aggravated harassment, a misdemeanor, at the court office. Mary went to the court office
and told her story to the complaint clerk. Although an
arrest could have been made, the clerk suggested an
alternative to arrest. Mary didn't want to harm Blue or
have him put in jail; she just wanted to be left alone.
The complaint clerk recommended arbitration or mediation through the center for dispute settlement. A counselor would meet with Mary and Larry and would try to
make the young man realize that the relationship was
over. The counselor also would help the couple work out
an agreement to resolve their differences and demand
that Larry leave Mary alone. If either person broke the
agreement, an aggravated harassment charge could be
tried in court or a financial penalty imposed.*

Centers for dispute settlement, which are nationwide, are
very effective in diverting cases from arrest and prosecution. Instead, they are handled in a swift, efficient,
professional manner by an independent, well-trained arbitrator, or mediator. The setting is informal and there
are no legalities. Lawyers are not needed.

In an arbitration an impartial third party hears both sides of a dispute and renders a decision that is binding on both sides. Mediation is a process of coming to an agreement with the assistance of a third party. Often, once there has been an arrest in cases involving relationships between former lovers, family members, neighbors, or other people who very much need to resolve their relationships, the judge or district attorney may suggest, or even order, this procedure in lieu of criminal prosecution.

In some cities district attorneys act as mediators. When a victim wants the police to arrest a person, the district attorney first calls for a pre-warrant hearing to try to work out the differences between the parties. Both pre-warrant hearings and centers for dispute settlement help achieve justice without arrest. This kind of assistance allows the courts to devote more time to more serious disputes that involve criminal penalties.

Other alternatives to arrest include

- pre-warrant hearings by the district attorney's office
- reference to centers for dispute settlement for arbitration or mediation

Not all cases of obscene phone calls are handled as simply as Mary's was. If you do not know the person who is calling, you can notify the police or the telephone company to tap your line. Eventually you will learn who is calling, and the police can follow through. This type of aggravated harassment results in an actual arrest by the

police and prosecution by the district attorney. You should
not acknowledge obscene phone calls by staying on the
line or talking to the person who is trying to make conversation with you. Women whose names are listed in
the phone book receive a high percentage of these calls.
Police advise the use of first initials for a woman's name
instead of a full name in the directory. If you should
receive calls that upset you, report them to the police or
telephone company at once.

OTHER MISDEMEANORS
AND PETTY OFFENSES

There are many other types of arrests for misdemeanors
and petty offenses. Disorderly conduct and fights, inter-
fering with a police officer (called obstructing govern-
mental administration), assault on a police officer, misconduct of officials, bribery, prostitution, and witness
tampering are other examples. The cases described, however, give you an idea of how two typical cases may be
handled.

Misdemeanors and petty offenses deluge the court system. If you file a charge or request a police officer to
make an arrest, be prepared to follow through or your
case will be lost in the shuffle. Know the result you want
to obtain. For example, are you interested in being paid
for the damages you suffered? Are you seeking an arrest
to help the defendant obtain needed help or counseling?
Is punishment the best result? Whatever goal you wish,
be certain your views are known by the district attorney.

PART II
THE CRIMES

CHAPTER 6

PERSONAL CRIMES OF VIOLENCE

Every hour an average of 150 violent crimes are committed throughout the United States. In such crimes a person willfully intends the death or injury, or the threat of force or violence, to another person. Examples are murder, aggravated assault, robbery, and rape.*

These crimes are personal in nature because the victim is forced into a face-to-face confrontation with the attacker. Very often weapons—handguns, rifles, pistols, knives, and clubs—are used by the attacker. While financial loss frequently occurs as a result of the crimes, the true impact of violent crimes on the system cannot be measured in monetary terms. The impact of death, disabling injuries, and emotional scars are not calculable.

---

* Because of the special nature of rape, it is the subject of an entire chapter (7).

MURDER

Though they had been college sweethearts, Ezra and Betty Flip had a marriage that was violent for most of its thirteen years. One day Ezra, who had been away on a business trip, arrived home unannounced and two days earlier than expected. When he observed a strange car in the driveway, he quickly concluded that it was owned by a man who was visiting Betty. Ezra rushed into their home, surprising Betty in the kitchen. Without asking a single question, Ezra grabbed a kitchen knife and stabbed his wife fifteen times in the chest. Betty had no time to explain that she had borrowed a friend's car because her own needed repairs.

Harold Sheldon woke up at 5:30 A.M. as he had every workday for fifteen years. He left his wife and two sleeping children and headed to the bus stop at the end of the block. A youth with knife in hand approached Harold at the bus stop and demanded money. Too proud to give in readily, Harold pushed the boy away. Within seconds, Harold was stabbed to death.

On a hot summer day Patrick Gunn, dressed in army fatigues and carrying a rifle, walked into his mother's home. After provoking a brief argument with a workman who was hanging wallpaper in the kitchen, Patrick shot and killed him. He then fled out the door and down the street, striking two passers-by with random shots. Moments later he rushed into a bank and ordered customers and bank personnel to lie on the floor. He fired at random again, killing a young woman teller and seriously injuring a customer. During the ensuing two-hour siege, he also seriously injured a number of police officers. When it was over, Patrick Gunn lay dead, too, slain with a single bullet fired by a police marksman.

Murder, the willful killing of one human being by another, takes many forms. In 1981 there were 22,516 murders reported in the United States. Murders associated with robberies, rape, and drugs account for the loss of thousands of lives each year. However, the largest classification involves victims who have been friends or relatives of the murderer. Nearly 55 percent of murder victims in 1981 were acquainted with their assailant.

Ezra Flip ended the violence in his marriage with the murder of his wife. His case was not untypical. More than 8.5 percent of the murders committed in 1981 were by one spouse against the other. An additional 8 percent of murders that year were committed by other family members. Such cases often involve jealousies, longstanding ill feelings, or money.

A recent case that aroused national attention was the death of diet doctor Herman Tarnower. The millionaire doctor had ended his relationship with a woman named Jean Harris after a ten-year romance. The jilted lover, who had been replaced by a younger woman, confronted the doctor in his Westchester County, New York, mansion. She was later convicted of shooting him twice with a handgun.

Murders of individuals involved in romantic triangles are reported nationwide more than ten times each week.

Law enforcement officials have little or no control in preventing murders within families or murders related to romantic triangles. However, such crimes create victims among the survivors. The crimes are just as important to society as those committed during robberies and other felonies.

In cases like Patrick Gunn's, no motive can be addressed. Such multiple murderers exhibit deranged and troubled minds and leave in their trail shocking results and bewildered survivors.

Harold Sheldon was murdered by a person intending to commit a different crime. In the attempt to rob Harold of his money, the youth became annoyed. His instant reaction was to use a knife, an action that caused Harold's death. Many murders occur during the commission of another felony.

Police Investigations

Police authorities assign top priority to murder investigations. Special homicide squads exist in nearly all police departments and prosecutors' offices. In the court system, too, this type of crime is often given priority. Seventy-two percent of all murders nationwide are solved by police authorities.

Police rely on eyewitness accounts, technical evidence gathered at the scene, and other information from the investigation to develop a motive and a relationship between the victim and the murderer. Often informants— community members used by the police to provide information about the area's criminal network—come forward to volunteer information.

The individuals involved in the prosecution of alleged murders are often the most competent members of the district attorney's staff. Many police departments use the best-trained police officers and newest scientific methods of gathering evidence.

Who Are the Victims?

Overlooked in the catastrophe of murder are the survivors, whose first task it is to bury the dead. Survivors frequently question the murder, unable to understand why there *was* a murder. They may experience guilt, believing they could have done something to prevent the death. They live with fear of reprisal and fear that the crime may be repeated. Frequently survivors alter their living patterns as a result of a murder.

Survivors often have a difficult time coping. Little attention is paid to a surviving spouse, parent, or other family member because prosecutors are primarily interested in eyewitnesses, technical evidence, and in seeing that the assailant is arrested and convicted. Family members who are not part of that process often feel left out and isolated.

If you are a survivor, you have rights. You should contact the police and the prosecutor's office and demand that additional protection be given to you for as long as necessary. While you are at the funeral, insist that your house be watched by local police to prevent a burglary

by someone who knows you are away. Tell the prosecutors in writing what your feelings are concerning the
prosecution of the defendant. Notify the judge by letter
that you are interested in the case. Be prepared to attend
the trial. Talk to the prosecutor about your presence in
the courtroom. You should be made aware of the rights
of defendants and that a person charged with murder who
enters a plea of not guilty is presumed innocent until
proven guilty by the district attorney. This legal requirement may require several hearings and many months to
reach a final result. Ask the district attorney exactly what
course the case will follow. Many cases are fraught with
legal difficulties, so inquire about potential problems.

When there is a conviction, be sure to contact either
the judge or the Probation Department. Let them know
the extent of your loss and your feelings about the case.

In dealing with officials, victims should

- understand that the police must gather information
  and evidence to ready a case for trial
- contact police officers and the district attorney for
  information
- inform officials that they want to be involved in the
  process
- notify the district attorney of their willingness to be
  present in court
- request protection if required and seek protection
  for their house when they are away

- inform the Probation Department regarding their feelings toward the defendant when he or she admits guilt
- understand the legal difficulties in prosecution by discussing them with the district attorney

Dealing with Emotional Problems

The death of a person close to you is neither easily understood nor readily accepted. No explanation is sufficient. It is important that a murder victim's family seek psychological counseling. Counseling provides some comfort to assist you through a devastating period and helps reorient you and your family to life. Failure to acknowledge a need for counseling can result in deep hostility and anger, which can build to a dangerous point—and affect your future. Counseling is available in most communities and is provided by self-help groups and community mental health centers. You may be referred by your own physician or the victims' assistance division of your local police department or prosecutor's office.

Robert and Charlotte Hullinger lost their 19-year-old daughter when she was murdered in Germany by a hammer-wielding ex-boyfriend. Through a series of events following the tragedy, they founded a group called Parents of Murdered Children, which has established a nationwide network to help bereaved parents. Chapters located throughout the country offer help to any person who has lost a child of any age to murder. Chapter members offer support and friendship and provide information about grieving and the criminal justice system as it pertains to particular cases. By meeting with parents who have experienced similar recent tragedies, survivors have found fresh hope and reason for living. Such survivors realize that everyone who grieves needs a support system.

The reality is that the life of a murdered person cannot be returned. Survivors want to be assured that the criminal never has another chance to hurt someone else. Often survivors insist on the maximum sentence. In most states life imprisonment can be imposed. In rare instances the death penalty is an option.

Be aware that even though a life sentence is imposed, our system of parole permits an unexpected and early release of a murderer.

Parole from a Life Sentence

Our prisons are overcrowded, and the public has been unwilling to spend additional money for more prisons. Because of severe space limitations, parole boards often seek out prisoners who can be paroled so that there is room for newcomers. Parole involves the release of a prisoner before his sentence has expired. The decision is often based on good behavior while in prison.

William Fain is now a prisoner in San Quentin prison. In 1967, while driving along a country road in the San Joaquin Valley in California, he flashed his headlights at a car in front of him until it pulled over. When the teenage driver got out, Fain killed him with a shotgun and then raped his two young female companions. Fain

*was convicted of these crimes and a third rape and drew
a life sentence. Recently, after a hearing, the California
parole board ordered Fain's release. The victims' families learned about this decision and notified the attorney
general's office in Sacramento. Together the families put
together a committee that sparked public outrage over
the decision to release Fain. A petition stating that Fain
was too dangerous to return to the community was signed
by 62,500 persons. City councils and county boards in
the surrounding areas and even the state legislature urged
parole officials to reconsider. As a result of such pressure, the decision to release Fain was reversed.*

Public outrage is never *legally* relevant, but it can exert
pressure on a parole board by bringing other factors into
consideration. This sort of public pressure is, however,
relatively new. In the past, many victims' families remained silent about decisions to parole because they feared
further victimization if they raised their voices.

People are growing increasingly cognizant of the power
of community organization in making the public aware
of the potential danger of releasing a person sentenced
to life imprisonment. Usually the goal is to exert pressure
on a parole board and to stir legislators to enact tougher
parole legislation.

Once assured that a convicted criminal will be removed
from society for life, victims should be able to relax. The
community's response to William Fain is one of many
taking place throughout the country—an appropriate response when parole boards decide to release prisoners
sentenced to life in prison.

A young girl named Pamela Moss was raped and murdered in the Rochester, New York, area. Her killer, who was sentenced to life in prison in 1963, is now a model prisoner and eligible for parole in the New York State corrections system. The family of the dead girl told the judge at the time of sentencing that they did not want the murderer of their child to be executed, despite the fact that executions were then common. Instead, they wanted only to be assured that he would be put away in a prison for life. So, they were unable to accept that the assailant, who had confessed to several rapes as well, was being considered for parole. The Moss family subsequently spoke to members of the press and enlisted the aid of thousands to ensure the continued incarceration of the assailant; the State Parole Board consequently denied release on parole for at least two years.

Compensation to Victims' Families

Medical bills incurred by a victim prior to death, often totaling thousands of dollars, must be paid. Burial and funeral expenses normally run to at least several thousand dollars.

Victim Harold Sheldon had supported a wife and two children. Mortgage payments and money for food, clothing, and miscellaneous items were all provided by him. Consequently, in addition to their emotional loss, his family suffered extreme financial loss. Expenses included the cost of counseling, psychological and psychiatric help, and job retraining for his wife.

Some people have life insurance, which pays a benefit when a person dies. In some cases, social security benefits may be available, and these may include a lump sum to defray burial costs. Social security for survivors, including a spouse or children under the age of 18, can be paid as an annuity for a specified period of time. In many cases, judges can order a defendant who is convicted to make restitution. If the murderer has funds, restitution can be completed at the time of sentencing.

A murderer's potential earnings or inheritances can be seized and diverted to the family of a victim. To do so, a *tort* action must be instituted against the defendant. Many survivors are now suing persons responsible for the deaths or injuries of other family members and receiving monetary judgments. Although in most cases judgments awarded by the court in civil actions may never be collected, a judgment stands as notice to all that any assets the defendant may acquire will be seized to benefit the victim's family.

Third-party actions are being used to a greater extent when attorneys believe a person, through negligence, has contributed to the death of the victim.

A tenant was attacked by a painter who had been given keys to all the apartments in the building. The landlord knew that the painter was dangerous, for he had been violent in the past. The landlord was negligent because he permitted the painter access to tenants' private living areas.

Victims' compensation programs have been created in thirty-eight states (see Appendix A). In each of those states lump-sum death benefits are paid to the survivors of a murder victim. In some cases compensation boards provide counseling services free of charge or the funds necessary to pay for such services. Many states provide a burial allowance to assist the family or funds for immediate expenses.

Survivors can be compensated through

- life insurance
- social security lump-sum death benefits
- social security payments to survivors, including surviving spouse and children
- court-ordered restitution
- legal action against murderer
- legal action against a third party who may have contributed to the murderer's action

ROBBERY

Traveling salesman John Brody had just checked into a downtown New York hotel. This was his first visit to the city. After a late dinner he took a walk and explored the area. After strolling for more than an hour, he turned off Fifth Avenue and walked down a dark side street, thinking it was a shortcut to the hotel. Suddenly two youths jumped in front of him and ordered, "Give us your money and your watch or you're dead." Immediately Brody handed over his wallet and took off his watch. The youths fled into the darkness.

The Elliott family lived in a large residence in suburban Westchester County, New York. Alice Strom, the housekeeper, opened the front door one afternoon to two men who asked, "Is this 287 Apple Way?" The housekeeper nodded. The men told her they were delivering a package. As she opened the locked screen door to accept the package, one man held the door as they both pushed into the house. They told Alice to be quiet, took her to the kitchen, and tied and gagged her so that she could not move or make a sound. In the next few minutes the two men made their rounds of the house looking for jewels, money, and other valuables. As they prepared to leave, 6-year-old Jason Elliott walked in the back door. The intruders grabbed the child and tied him next to Alice.

The two men rushed out, jumped into their van, and drove off. A neighbor, who had become suspicious, went to the Elliott home. He found both Alice and Jason unharmed and called the police. He gave a good description of the van and its license number. The police soon spotted it on a nearby highway.

Late one night Paul Ross was at his convenience grocery store readying the night deposit. A lone man walked in, brandished a revolver, and demanded all of Paul's money. Paul turned over the night deposit money and gave him his wallet as well. The bandit left as quickly as he had entered. Paul instantly pushed the silent alarm that alerted local police.

Robbery is the taking of, or the attempt to take, anything of value from another person's control. It is accomplished by force or the threat of force or violence. More than half of the 574,134 robberies reported in the United States in 1981 occurred on the street. Bank holdups, which draw greater publicity, accounted for only slightly more than 1 percent of the total. Most victims are ordinary people, who, like John Brody, Alice, Jason, and Paul, are interrupted in their daily routines. The primary motive in robbery cases is to get away with property, usually cash, jewelry, or other valuables.

A robbery involves a face-to-face confrontation between the victim and the robber. A robbery is distinguished from a burglary, where an item of value may be taken after a break-in of a building. A gun, knife, or club is often used in a robbery. Other times no weapon is shown, but the person being robbed is made to believe that he or she will be harmed by a weapon or physical force if the robber's orders are not followed.

Bodily harm is a threat robbers make and occasionally carry through. Often this depends on how the robber views his own safety during the crime. Your reaction may be the determining factor. No resistance was offered by the victims mentioned above, and they did not get hurt. Many people are not as fortunate.

If you find yourself a victim in a robbery, don't panic. Keep cool. Usually the robber does not want to harm you. He only wants your property. If you frighten him, you may trigger an attack.

Attempt to escape if it is practical. However, a robber usually makes escape difficult. They prefer to choose situations where few, if any, witnesses can view their actions. If you are asked for money, hand it over. Some people actually carry two wallets, one of which contains only a few dollars. Their actual identification, credit cards, and most of their money is kept in the second wallet.

During a robbery, carefully observe the robber's characteristics, especially any unusual features. Note clothing, including the type of shoes, and specifically note any facial characteristics such as a beard, large nose, or birthmark. Is the robber wearing glasses?

After you have complied with the robber's request, the robber usually leaves quickly. Do not try to block the robber's exit or be a hero. Such actions only lead to harm. When the robber leaves, seek safety immediately and contact the police. If you use a telephone, call the operator or, if applicable, the emergency number, 911. State exactly where you are and what happened. You will be connected with the proper police department. Tell the police operator that you have just been held up. Identify your location and answer briefly any questions you are asked. Follow the police operator's directions. An officer will come to your assistance. You will then be asked several questions and to describe the robber in detail. Try to remember exactly what property was taken and describe unusual characteristics of the property.

If you are confronted by a robber

- do not panic
- remember, a robber's main objective is not to hurt you but to steal your property

- attempt escape *only* if it is practical
- do not offer resistance; give the robber the property he seeks
- do not frighten the robber
- do not block the exit or try to be a hero
- carefully note the robber's appearance, including his clothing and any unusual characteristics
- immediately seek safety
- contact the police
- notify the police operator of your location and briefly describe the incident
- answer the police operator's questions briefly
- wait for police officer to arrive
- describe the incident and the property you lost

Some 24 percent of robbery offenses reported to law enforcement officials in 1981 were solved. Factors that increase the likelihood of apprehension and arrest include an immediate report of the incident; an accurate description of the robber; eyewitness accounts, and very specific property identification. Once you've reported a robbery, be prepared and willing to make further identification of the robber. You may be asked to view mug shots of several suspects. You may also be asked to view a lineup. You should give police your address and phone number and an alternate number where you can be reached. You may also be called to testify at a preliminary hearing within a few days of any arrest. In addition, you may have to testify at a grand jury hearing and again at the time of trial.

The police will ask you to

• describe the incident
• make a list of your property
• identify the suspect from photographs or a lineup
• inform them of where you can be reached
• be prepared to testify at a preliminary hearing, the grand jury, and the trial

If the suspected robber is arrested, what can you expect in terms of court appearances, return of your property, and prevention of a similar occurrence? You should discuss these questions thoroughly with the investigating officer and find out which member of the district attorney's office is in charge of the case. Feel free to contact both the police and the district attorney's office frequently. When you are asked for your phone number, be sure you get the officials' business phone numbers.

Financial Loss

Bessie Sax walked down a dark street at 6 A.M. en route to her job as a criminal court clerk. Suddenly she felt a rush from behind. A youth grabbed her purse from her arm and ran away with it. As he pushed by her, she fell down and broke her glasses. Bessie was the victim of a purse-snatching robbery. Her purse contained the key to her house and her car keys, for which she had no duplicates. In addition, Bessie lost several major credit cards, her driver's license, cash, personal letters, photographs, sales receipts, and important personal documents, including her passport.

Much later, she jokingly revealed that she had enough items in her purse to take a trip to Europe. Now she advises women to check their purses periodically to determine what they're carrying. You'll find, she says, you don't need 75 percent of what you put in your purse. Also, she adds, be sure you have copies or identifying numbers of important items so that you can immediately contact banks, the Motor Vehicle Department, and anyone else who may be affected by the theft. A person who seizes a purse or wallet may attempt to use your credit cards and your identification. In some cases a person stopped for a traffic violation has handed another person's license to the investigating officer. A ticket was written in the name on the operator's license. When the victim did not appear in court to answer the traffic violation, his license was suspended. If you do not notify the Motor Vehicle Department of your loss, you may become a victim several times over.

Many people carry much too much cash on their person. Consider how much you actually will need during your daily travels and keep only that amount with you.

Victims' compensation boards, which were discussed earlier, may be an appropriate remedy for obtaining financial relief. Victims' assistance groups also provide help. In some cases, emergency funds for such items as broken glasses may be available. If there is an arrest following a robbery and the police do not recover the stolen goods, the judge may order the defendant to make restitution as part of his sentence.

Prevention

Many robberies can be prevented. John Brody has the right to walk down any street, but in the future he will be much more careful. Not only will he be aware of the presence of other people, he will take his future walks in lighted areas. He also will carry only the cash he really needs.

Bessie will be much more aware of people walking behind her when she's on her way to work. She'll park her car in a well-lit area. If somebody is walking behind her, she will wait until they pass so that she will not be surprised.

Alice Strom will not open the door for a stranger, no matter what they tell her. Instead, she will instruct the stranger to leave the package by the front door.

Paul Ross will not total his store's night deposit in plain view of the street. Instead, he will lock the doors and go into the back room.

Realize that not everyone around you has kind motives. Take steps to protect yourself against potential robberies.

To prevent robberies,

- always be *aware* of a danger
- do not display valuables (i.e., jewelry, money) while walking down the street
- do not let a stranger into your home without identification
- do not walk in dark areas alone
- be careful of the situations in which you put yourself

AGGRAVATED ASSAULT

An attack by one person against another for the purpose
of inflicting severe bodily injury is an aggravated assault.
In 1981, 643,720 aggravated assaults were reported to
law enforcement officials. In three-quarters of these
crimes, a weapon was used, most commonly a handgun
or a knife.

Very often the victim knows the attacker. The motives
for the crime are similar to those outlined for murder
cases. A reaction to an argument, the culmination of a
long-standing feud, and a determination to get revenge
are all motives for aggravated assault. There are many
cases, however, in which the assault occurred during the
commission of another crime. A robbery or burglary can
become a case of aggravated assault when the victim is
seriously injured.

*Alvin Burger and his wife, Carol, were visiting the Boston
area for the weekend to attend their daughter's gradu-
ation from law school. After a late dinner, the couple
were directed to a well-lit parking garage. From there,
they understood, a bus would take them to their hotel.
However, the Burgers had missed the last bus. The garage attendant assured them that the way to their hotel
was well-lit and that they should not be fearful; it was
summer and many people were still out and about at
midnight.*

*As Alvin and Carol walked down Beacon Street, they
felt a sense of security. People strolled nearby, and jog-
gers passed them frequently. As they turned into another*

street near their hotel, they noticed a shadowy, dark area they would have to pass. As they approached it, two young men emerged and struck a karate stance. Instinctively, Alvin stopped, clutching a shoe box he had under his arm. Carol ran toward the middle of the street screaming to attract attention. Alvin, however, was clubbed several times and suffered serious injury.

Carol was unable to run for help because she was grabbed and pushed down. Soon after, passengers in a taxi cab ordered the driver to stop; they picked up Alvin and Carol and drove them to a nearby hospital.

This was a case of attempted robbery in which the robbers became frightened and reacted with their clubs. In that instant, Alvin's life changed significantly. He was disabled for three months; years later he still suffers terrible physical and emotional side effects. For her part, Carol refuses to go out alone and is fearful of young people with characteristics similar to those of the two attackers.

Police were unsuccessful in solving the case. Alvin filed a claim with the Victims of Violent Crime Compensation in the state of Massachusetts. The administrator of the compensation board took the position that out-of-state residents were not protected by Massachusetts law. The Burgers were victims of both the crime and the system. Alvin and Carol Burger's daughter has filed a lawsuit against the Massachusetts compensation board to have their claim considered. The Burgers' suit claims that all people within the state, not just residents, have the right to be compensated when they are victims of crime.

In most cases, as the victim of an assault, you may file a claim with the victims' compensation board in the state where you were assaulted. Although the Burgers encountered administrative difficulties, most victims *will* be compensated.

Whether you are the survivor of a murder victim or the victim of a robbery or aggravated assault, you can obtain financial compensation. Know all your options. Investigate victims' compensation boards, laws administered by the state, court-ordered restitution, and legal action against the perpetrator of a personal crime of violence.

CHAPTER 7
RAPE

Maria, a 19-year-old college freshman, went to the One Thousand Club, a local disco, to meet friends and dance. Early in the evening, a nice looking, personable young man named Steve struck up a conversation with her. He asked her to dance several times and seemed more than a little aggressive. Maria noticed that he followed her every time she moved on to talk to someone else. Late in the evening, while she was with several other friends, Maria agreed to dance with him again. Steve asked repeatedly for her phone number. Just as she was ready to leave with her friends, he pleaded one more time for her number. Flattered by his persistence, she gave it to him. The following day Steve called and asked her if she would like to spend the evening dancing at the One Thousand Club. Maria agreed. As they drove away from her house, Steve told her he had forgotten his wallet and had to return home. Upon arriving at his apartment, Steve invited Maria in, warning her that it was not safe to stay in the car alone. She followed him upstairs and into the apartment. Once they were inside the door, he reached back, secured the dead bolt, turned the key, and removed it. Maria felt trapped and instantly realized something was wrong—very wrong. She was grabbed, forced to the floor, and raped continuously for what seemed like hours. Later, telling Steve she had to use the bathroom, she flung open the window and jumped two stories, sustaining critical injuries.

Fourteen-year-old Jody was attending a party several blocks from her home. She had gone to the party against her parents' wishes. When darkness fell, the party ended and Jody found she did not have a ride home. She called her father, but he was still annoyed with her and told her she would have to walk. It was a warm, pleasant night. Jody didn't notice she was being followed. Three blocks from the party someone clapped a hand over her mouth and dragged her behind some bushes next to a commercial building. A young man forced her at knife point to commit sexual acts, then left her sprawled helplessly on the ground but did not otherwise harm her.

Margaret, a 78-year-old widow, walked the two blocks to her church every day. One cold winter day she was grabbed from behind and pulled into an automobile, where she was raped and severely beaten by a youth.

Rape is a violent crime. It is not an act in which the rapist seeks sexual gratification but a crime of assault in which the attacker singles out a victim to act out his anger against society.

In 1981, 81,536 forcible rapes were reported in the United States. Many thousands more were not reported to authorities. Any female, regardless of age, race, or economic status, may become a victim of rape. Contrary to old myths, rape victims do not "ask for it," nor do they "enjoy" being raped. Neither the way a woman walks nor the clothes she wears affects the incidence of rape.

A rapist cannot be identified by his outward appearance. He may pose as a delivery man, repair man, or salesman. He could be a blind date, casual acquaintance, or anyone else. However, rapists are not ordinary, normal, functioning males. Rapists are individuals with major deficiencies in their personalities.

Studies generally classify three types of rapists. Most are *power* rapists. Because they need to build their egos and emphasize their masculinity, they select women who appear to be weak. Usually their rape victims are threatened but not otherwise physically harmed.

The *anger* rapist lashes out at the wrongs he believes all women in his life have caused. Maybe a teacher, his mother, or grandmother suppressed him. The reasons an anger rapist acts are numerous. This type of rapist can cause physical injury to his victim.

A third and less common type of rapist is labeled a *sadist*. His rape is ritualistic. His victims may be burned or carved or otherwise mutilated. Victims of this type of rapist are often young children.

The most publicized type of rape is the surprise attack at home, on a street, or in a park. Many rapes, including

Jody's, occur in just these ways. Yet almost half the rape victims reported in 1981 were acquainted with their rapist. Rapists may try to lure their victims into a casual friendship, just as Steve lured Maria.

WHAT TO DO IF
YOU ARE ATTACKED

If you find yourself confronted with the threat of an immediate rape attack, you must consider different tactics. Each situation will be different, depending on the surroundings, your attitude and personality, and the attacker's reaction. Rapists often select as their targets women who are easily intimidated or who appear helpless or unsure of themselves. Such individuals are least likely to resist their attackers. If you are confronted, you should appear determined, competent, and assertive.

Try to communicate by talking naturally. Don't cry or beg. Speak calmly. Such a response may reduce the rapist's rage and enhance his ego. You may also stall to gain time to recover from the initial shock and survey your predicament. You may do the unexpected, such as telling him you have venereal disease or that you are having a menstrual period. You may pretend to faint or feign severe pains.

You must consider carefully whether to run or scream. Run only if you are sure you can get to a safe place. Your screams may frighten off the rapist, but they may also stir him to violence. You are more likely to scare your assailant if you use a whistle or shrill alarm.

Once you decide to fight, you are committed to that course. You must win the fight. If you have weapons, such as keys, combs, hatpins, or even hair spray or mace, use them if you can. You may be successful, but remember that your weapons might be turned on you. If no alternative is available, you may have to submit to the rapist to avoid serious injury. Evaluate your situation as carefully as possible and determine what the results of your action might be.

If you are attacked,

- stall by talking calmly to the attacker and use the time to think of a plan
- have confidence in your conversation. Be assertive
- scream and run only if you can reach a safe place quickly
- fight if you must, but be sure you are going to win the fight
- submit in order to avoid serious injury if you have no other alternative

WHAT TO DO IF YOU ARE RAPED

If you are raped, you will undoubtedly feel shock, fear, and perhaps guilt. You may blame yourself, thinking that you could have avoided the rape. This reaction is common, and may lead to a decision not to report the rape. Many women fear additional humiliation if they seek help within the legal system. Many also feel a sense of total isolation.

You should always report a rape. You have been assaulted and violated. Call the police immediately. Tell the operator you have been raped and give your location. A police officer will respond quickly. The officer's immediate tasks are to quickly obtain information about the attack, to preserve the crime scene, and to obtain medical help for you. It makes no difference whether a male or female police officer responds. And remember that the officer has a job to perform, that is, to get the facts immediately; his or her questions are not intended to be cold and compassionless though they may appear to be.

As a rape victim, one of your first reactions may be that you feel dirty, that you must bathe immediately. *Don't do it.* You will destroy evidence that will be valuable in apprehending your attacker. Do not change your clothes, douche, or clean up. Do not use any medication or urinate. At the hospital, the police officer may ask for your clothing. The officer will make arrangements for you to obtain clean clothes. The police are looking for semen, pubic hair, and other physical evidence.

If you are raped,

- immediately report the rape to the police
- answer the police officer's questions briefly and to the point
- seek immediate medical attention, but do not bathe, clean up, or douche
- do not change your clothes

When you discuss the case with the police officer, be as clear as possible in your description of the attacker.

The description of your attacker should include

- car license, make, and model
- race of assailant
- any pitch or accent to his voice
- approximate age, weight, and height
- description of clothing
- color and length of hair
- color of eyes
- any unusual marks, scars, tattoos, or jewelry
- missing teeth

After you've been raped, begin to build a support system immediately. Call a close friend and have that person stay with you. Contact a rape crisis service in your community. A trained counselor will come to your assistance immediately and remain with you for as long as necessary. If you do not have a community program, call the Rape Crisis Service 24-hour hotline, which is available in most communities. You may ask a police officer to call for you. (Appendix B lists 141 of the rape crisis services available in the United States.)

After you have been examined in a hospital, police officers may ask you to look at photographs of persons matching the description of your assailant. Carefully review the photos and select one *only* if you believe it to be of your assailant. A police technician will then use a special kit to create a sketch that will reflect the description you have given. The composite sketch is created from your description of eyebrows, nose, eyes, shape of facial features, hair, and soon it is a most useful tool in identifying a suspect.

You may also be asked to look at several persons in a lineup. One-way mirrors or special windows prevent persons in the lineup from seeing you.

A prompt report to the police assists in the apprehension of your attacker. After the initial police interrogation and identification, in many cases a detective will contact you with follow-up questions.

To recover from a rape, you need continuing support. You have been viciously and personally violated. Talk about it with a close friend or with the counselor provided by your rape crisis center. And remember that your rapist is not a typical man—he is an unusual, sick criminal.

Police make arrests in 48 percent of known forceable rapes in this country. Once you have made your complaint, you will have to sign statements. Carefully review them for accuracy. You will be tested on your statements when you testify later in court.

If a suspect is arrested, he will be taken before a judge. The district attorney will attempt to keep him in custody. As with any other crime, a defendant arrested for rape is entitled to very specific rights. Such rights include the right to a lawyer and the right to be released prior to a conviction.

When a person charged enters a "not guilty" plea, the legal presumption of innocence cloaks him until and unless the district attorney proves him guilty at a trial. The entry of a not guilty plea does not mean that the defendant is claiming he did not do the act. Our legal system requires the district attorney and the accuser to prove that the defendant committed the act. As the accuser, you become part of the process. You may testify at the preliminary hearing, which is held to determine whether the defendant should continue in custody. Next, if required, you must be prepared to testify at a grand jury proceeding and a trial. Contact the district attorney and ask to be made aware of your responsibilities in prosecuting the case. Be sure to tell him or her where you can be reached. Feel free to ask all pertinent questions.

In dealing with the police

- give a specific description of the rapist
- try to identify the suspect from police photographs
- try to identify the suspect from a police lineup
- work with a police technician to create a composite sketch
- after the initial report, give any in-depth interviews required by detectives
- be prepared to testify at a preliminary hearing, grand jury, and trial
- feel free to discuss the case often with the prosecutor and district attorney

As a rape victim, you can expect the criminal justice system to be interested in the prosecution of your case; some of the best and most experienced prosecutors are assigned to rape cases.

COMPENSATION FOR INJURIES

Victims of rape usually suffer financial losses as a result of their injuries. In many states there is no fee for the initial medical exam after a rape. In some states counseling may be provided free or be paid for by victims' compensation programs. State programs usually compensate the victim for injuries. When sentencing a convicted rapist, a judge can require that the rapist provide restitution to the victim. A victim may also bring a lawsuit against a rapist.

A 15-year-old from Nebraska sued and won $22,500 from her attacker. She punished the rapist by using the system. Such lawsuits are usually successful and often result in the collection of funds. They also have a therapeutic value.

Third parties can also be held accountable in rape cases. A hotel owner in New Jersey failed to provide proper security for guests. He knew room locks were flimsy and had been broken before. A woman was attacked by a rapist during the night and a jury later brought in a verdict against the hotel owner for several thousand dollars. Other types of third-party actions are also available.

The compensation available to rape victims includes

- a medical examination
- counseling arranged through victims' compensation programs

- restitution by the rapist ordered by the court
- civil lawsuits against rapists
- third-party actions

AVOIDING RAPE

Most women will never be rape victims. However, all women should take preventive measures. Alert women avoid rape encounters. Be aware of yourself, your surroundings, and your capabilities.

To avoid a possible attack situation at home

- keep doors and windows secured
- install a peephole in your door
- have good lighting in your house and lights on in more than one room
- install dead-bolt locks
- refuse to let any stranger into your house to use your telephone; offer to make the call for him
- have a security check of your house by a police officer
- tell callers who want to know if you are alone that your husband's sleeping and doesn't want to be disturbed
- use your initials rather than your first name in the phone book and on the mailbox
- hang up immediately on obscene phone callers
- require delivery men to show identification

- get out of an elevator early if you feel uncomfortable with strangers on it

To avoid a possible
attack situation in your car

- keep the car doors locked, the windows up, and the car in good running order
- know where you are going and how to get there
- check your gas before each trip
- never pick up hitchhikers
- do not stop to aid a stranger; call the police for him
- raise the hood if you have car trouble and get back in the car. Through a small crack in the window, ask anyone who stops to call the police for you

If you believe somebody is following you, do not try to attract attention. Do not go home. Instead, go to a fire station or police station or an all-night grocery—any place where you'll find people. Park your car near your destination in a well-lighted area. Lock your car and always have your keys ready when you return. When you're going out, let somebody know where you're going and when you expect to be home. Don't walk alone at night if at all possible. If you do walk home late at night, vary your route each time. Walk facing oncoming traffic. If you are harassed by an occupant of a car, simply turn around and walk the other way. When you return home always have your key ready.

When meeting men for the first time be careful not to put yourself in a situation such as Maria encountered with

Steve. Be wary of new acquaintances who suddenly wish to be helpful and alone with you. Go out with friends in a group and stay with them throughout your first encounters with other men. Talk with people who have known a man socially before you put yourself in a vulnerable situation. By using your head and being aware at all times, you can avoid confrontations.

RAPE CRISIS SERVICES

Many private and publicly funded organizations have been developed to assist victims of sexual assault. In almost every community in the country, 24-hour hotlines are available to assist such victims. Appendix B provides numbers of many of those hotlines.

Rape crisis service personnel provide valuable assistance to the rape victim. At your first call a trained person is sent to be with you. Initially, that person is concerned with offering compassion and helping you obtain medical information and emotional support. The next step is to guide you through the complete legal process—from the initial police interview through trial. Rape crisis service personnel will explain the court process and the realities of your case. Counselors explain to your family what you are going through. They will also refer you and your family to professionals for additional counseling. The rape crisis service considers the men in your life who will be affected by your rape; your husband, boyfriend, father, or child will receive any necessary assistance or counseling.

Third-party reporting is often available to rape victims. If you do not wish to report a rape yourself, you might be able to report everything but your name to a rape hotline. When a suspect is apprehended, you will then be advised of your responsibilities to come forward and press charges.

Other groups, such as political action groups, are primarily interested in changing rape-related legislation. You may or may not be interested in such a service. Be careful to select the type of assistance that will provide the services you want.

NEW ATTITUDES BENEFIT RAPE VICTIMS

Attitudes toward rape victims have changed in the last several years, and it is hoped that these changes will encourage rape victims to report their attacks.

Recently, in Connecticut, a bill was passed that makes it more difficult for attorneys representing defendants in rape cases to raise issues regarding a victim's prior sexual history. In Michigan, a new law prohibits police officers from requiring victims to take lie detector tests before they can press charges. In California, new sentencing laws for rapes have resulted in a tripling of the time to which rapists are sentenced. New York State has passed a law eliminating the need for the prosecution to show clear signs of "earnest resistance" or injury to a nonsexual part of the victim's body. At the same time that the law was on the books, law enforcement authorities had been advising women not to struggle during a rape for fear the attacker would be provoked into violent action. This contradiction is now eliminated. The new law requires that the victim's lack of consent, which is necessary proof for rape cases, be shown only through a threat of force or violence.

Many other states have changed laws to encourage victims to report rapes. In many areas citizens now patrol areas and distribute literature to educate people about rape. The public has reacted when light sentences have been given to rapists. In Massachusetts a judge sentenced five young men who admitted guilt in a gang rape to a period of probation; the subsequent public outrage prompted the judge to announce a new and stricter sentence based on new considerations.

The best way to deal with rape, however, is to prevent it. The best advice is to be vigilant, prepared, and to anticipate potential problems.

If you do become a victim, report the crime and immediately seek emotional support and assistance from rape crisis personnel and understanding authorities. Only if you report and prosecute can you attain justice both for yourself and your community.

CHAPTER 8
PROPERTY CRIMES

Every three seconds a property crime is committed somewhere in the United States. Ninety percent of all reported crime, in fact, involves burglaries, larceny-thefts, motor vehicle thefts, and incidents of vandalism.

Most of these crimes are impersonal. The person who commits the act usually does not know the victim, and face-to-face contact between them does not take place. The victim's chief problems are financial loss, inconvenience, and annoyance. With the exception of residential burglaries, where a significant amount of personal trauma is involved, these crimes are classified as low priority in the criminal justice system because there is no physical injury to the victim.

BURGLARY

Tom and Beth Izod were returning to their northern community after a wonderful midwinter week in Florida. Al-

though they had enjoyed their vacation, both were anxious to get home to the security and comfort of familiar surroundings.

As she walked into their home, Beth screamed. The cabinet doors in her kitchen and dining room were open and their personal belongings were scattered throughout the house. In that one instant the feelings of security they had always felt in their own home were destroyed. Tom and Beth had become victims.

The Financial Loss

In 1981 alone there were more than 3.7 million burglaries, and more than two-thirds of these occurred in residential properties—private homes, apartments, and condominiums. Property losses in that one year alone were estimated at $3.5 billion, according to the United States Department of Justice Uniform Crime Report. Any unlawful entry of a structure with the intention to commit a felony or theft is considered a burglary.

Many burglars are repeat offenders who have committed many break-ins in the same area. They move rapidly, strike at residences when no one is home, obtain items that are readily saleable, and fence or sell them quickly. The average dollar loss per burglary was $924 in 1981.

The theft of your belongings, however, may be only a part of your financial loss. Your home may be damaged. Burglars often break doors and windows to gain entry. Vandalism often goes hand in hand with burglary. Homes are ransacked, paint is sprayed on walls, and items are broken.

In the winter, when a window is smashed or a door is left open by a burglar at work in a vacant home, water pipes freeze, heating systems are affected, and consequential damages are exceedingly high. Some burglars even start fires to cover up burglaries.

When you are a burglary victim, it is difficult to assess accurately the time costs involved in repairing the damage, replacing the stolen items, and dealing with authorities. Your out-of-pocket costs may include telephone and transportation expenses and lost work time.

Financial losses resulting from burglaries include

- stolen items
- damage resulting from entry
- vandalism inside the structure
- consequential loss, such as broken water pipes
- lost work time and the inconvenience involved in trying to restore and replace missing items

The Emotional Upset

But financial loss is only part of the trauma a burglary victim experiences. A stranger has violated the homeowner's privacy. Irreplaceable personal belongings, private letters, and family heirlooms of little value to a burglar have been disturbed and are often missing or damaged. Fear, guilt, anger, insecurity, and a desire for revenge are common reactions, and they can consume an overwhelming amount of a victim's time and energy. Sometimes the victim has an extreme reaction to the trauma resulting from a burglary. Betty's case is a good example.

Betty and her husband had just purchased a new home in a suburb of a city in Virginia. One day she came home from shopping, opened her front door, and found a man in her living room. Betty turned and ran back out to the front porch, but the intruder followed, caught up with her, and shoved her to the ground. Fortunately a police officer who was passing by heard the commotion. He scared the intruder away but was unable to catch him. Betty, who was thoroughly undone by the incident, adamantly refused to enter her home again, and her husband was forced to put it up for sale.

Betty's reaction might have been less severe if she had sought counseling through her community mental health center. She could have been directed by the center to a professional skilled in dealing with the rehabilitation of crime victims.

When You Discover a Burglary

If you discover your home has been burglarized, do not enter unless you are certain that the intruder has left. Go to the nearest telephone where you can safely call the police. Do not disturb the crime scene in any way, or valuable evidence may be lost. When the police arrive, deal with the officer who is in charge of the investigation. The questions you will be asked are detailed in Chapter 4.

The police officers will take fingerprints and photographs and do other necessary identification work. They may talk to your neighbors to see if anyone noticed anything unusual. For your part, you will have to provide them with a list of missing items. If the list will be a long one, the police will often make a notation of the types of items missing and the approximate total value; it then becomes your responsibility to provide them with a detailed list—at a later date—including all the specifics you can remember: special marks, dates, initials, names, and the approximate value of each item. This is frequently a difficult task, for you may not discover that an item is missing for several days. It may be helpful to look at recent photographs taken inside your house. You should file your list of missing items as quickly as possible, of course, and it is imperative that you identify it with the case number, which the police will give you before they leave. This number is also essential for insurance companies and the IRS; the latter frequently investigates casualty loss claims (deductions) and will certainly check with the police if they feel they need verification.

After the initial police investigation you may never hear about your case again. Only 14 percent of the burglaries reported are actually cleared by the police. The intruders at the Izods, the couple whose house was burglarized while they vacationed in Florida, and at Betty's new home were never identified.

Burglary investigations that result in arrest fit into three basic categories. First, apprehension and arrest are very likely if an intruder is caught in the act and second, if the burglar and victim had some prior knowledge of one another (for example, acquaintances, employees, neighborhood youths). The third and most common type occurs when police apprehend a burglar and, in the course of interrogation, he admits to other burglaries.

Victims of burglaries usually have considerable difficulty in obtaining follow-up information about the crime. Because of the large volume of cases, police officers may not have the time to get back to you and tell you how the investigation is progressing. You must take the initiative and contact the investigating officer on your own. If you do not get the information you seek or are told your investigating officer is not available, ask for his sergeant or superior officer. If you persist, you will get the information.

In all likelihood you will fear being burglarized again. As the police explained to both Betty and the Izods, there are a number of simple steps you can take to prevent another burglary.

To prevent burglaries,

- put secure dead-bolt locks on your doors and use them even when you're home
- ask the police to check your house periodically while you're waiting for the new locks to be installed; unless you make a special request, this may not be done
- lock all windows securely when you go out; the installation of gates and bars on apartment windows that open on to fire escapes and terraces is an added precaution

- do not leave extra keys in the mailbox, on the windowsill, or under the doormat
- remove your car key from your key ring when someone borrows your car
- put a dolly bar at the bottom of sliding glass doors to prevent them from being opened
- keep window shades up so that your neighbors and the police can see into your home; however, where windows open on to fire escapes and terraces, keep the shades down
- keep the garage door locked at all times
- contact the police when you notice anything unusual in the neighborhood

When you go away

- notify your neighbors to watch for strangers around your house
- have your mail picked up by a friend or held at the post office
- stop the delivery of newspapers
- have the lawn mowed or snow shoveled regularly
- set an electrical timer to turn lights on in the evening and off in the morning
- remove any valuables from your house and store them in a safe deposit box at your bank
- do not leave money in your home

Victims worry most about being burglarized again when there has been no arrest. In such cases victims may become depressed and disillusioned with the criminal justice system. However, in those burglary cases where there *is* an arrest, some victims mistakenly take the attitude that, although they would like to participate in the system, nothing can be done.

Many others, however, fight back. They attempt to assist authorities in learning the identity of the culprit(s) and seeing that justice is done in the courts. All too often after an arrest has been made the court system moves slowly. Interested individuals and groups, however, have found that their input can ensure adequate treatment of their cases. The case of Punchy Albert is instructive.

Over the course of several months fifty-nine burglaries were committed in the Corn Hill area of Rochester, New York. Some houses were broken into two and even three times. After an extensive investigation, local police arrested Punchy Albert, 17, who admitted to numerous burglaries. At his arraignment, the court routinely released him on bail.

Neighborhood residents were so upset that they organized an association to accomplish two goals: to prevent crime and to ensure that justice was done in the court system when an arrest was made in their area.

One cold winter night shortly after Punchy was released on bail, Joe Audi heard the sound of breaking glass. When he found footprints leading to the back door of a house belonging to a neighbor who was away on vacation, he called the police. They arrived within two minutes and captured Punchy inside the home.

That same night the neighborhood association's security committee called an emergency meeting to for-

mulate a plan for informing the court of the neighborhood's concern. It was agreed the chairman of the committee would write a letter to the judge who was to arraign Punchy. The association wanted to let the court know that Punchy was a known burglar, was awaiting trial on other burglary charges, and that he appeared to be making a mockery of the criminal justice system.

The association's letter noted that Punchy chose the same houses over and over again. His victims were often elderly, and their fear of being burglarized had made them virtual prisoners in their own homes. In the letter the association called for a high cash bail and requested the case be expedited in the court system. The letter underscored the association's intent, stating, "We will have many of his victims in the courtroom to watch the Criminal Justice System in action, and we will follow this case very carefully through the courts." The chairman of the association attached to the letter a list of all the burglaries to which the defendant had admitted. The letter was delivered to the judge before Punchy's arraignment, and a copy was given to the district attorney.

At the 9:30 arraignment the next morning, nine people from the security committee took their places in the front row of the court. Many of them had taken time off from their jobs to be present.

When the case was called, the district attorney, who had already talked to both victims and neighborhood spokesmen, stated his reasons for opposing Punchy's release. After listening to the recommendations of the defense attorney and pretrial release personnel and after reading the neighborhood association's letter, the judge

*ordered the defendant held on high bail. He scheduled
a preliminary hearing three days later.*

*The district attorney, aware of the concern of the vic-
tims and their interest in prosecution, expedited the case
to the grand jury and quickly placed it on the trial calendar.*

*Within a few weeks, Punchy pleaded guilty to a charge
that resulted in a sentence of several years in the state
prison.*

*The Corn Hill Association had let its feelings and
concerns be known: They did not allow the case to be
treated as just one more burglary in the city. The judge
was impressed with the citizens' concern.*

*Within several months it was obvious that the asso-
ciation's tactics had a long-range effect. Word was out:
Corn Hill residents would not put up with crime in their
neighborhood. Burglars avoided the area, for the mes-
sage on the street was clear: If you get caught in Corn
Hill, you won't get out of jail easily. The mini crime wave
that had terrorized the neighborhood was over.*

The courts are swamped with cases, so the desire to
complete the court docket sometimes becomes more important than treating each case individually. The people
in the system know that victims often lose interest in
prosecuting a case. Ultimately, the case will be dismissed
if the victim does not testify. Rarely do victims appear
in court or show interest in following through by alerting
the district attorney and judge of their intent to participate
in the court process.

The Corn Hill neighbors had their case treated on a

personal, individual basis. In all cases a commitment to *follow through* is essential.

If you want restitution, ask the police or local victims' assistance unit for help. Stay informed of progress in your case. Find out whether witnesses and victims can be reimbursed for out-of-pocket expenses connected with court appearances.

The Corn Hill residents did not cease their activity when the Punchy Albert case was resolved. They instituted a neighborhood watch program. The State Crime Prevention Bureau and local police helped distribute pamphlets, instruction checklists, and window stickers, and assisted in organizing the neighborhood. If neighbors look out for one another and notice when something's amiss, the police can be notified quickly and the chances of apprehending intruders increased.

To get personal attention for your case

- notify the judge and district attorney by letter of your intent to appear in court (or at least your willingness to appear if required)
- determine whether there is a victims' assistance unit to help keep you informed
- ask the victims' assistance unit or the police how to seek restitution
- find out if there are services available to witnesses and victims, such as free parking, babysitting, and reimbursement for transportation expenses
- contact the investigating officer for updates on the progress of the case

Other Problems
Burglary Victims Face

Although an arrest was made in Punchy Albert's case, only 14 percent of all burglaries reported to the police are actually cleared, and arrests seldom occur. As a victim, your main task is to identify your specific damages and try to get some kind of restitution. If the police should apprehend the burglar, obtaining restitution from the person charged with the crime is obviously unlikely. Usually the defendant has committed several burglaries and restitution is just not possible. People who commit burglaries are often without funds to begin with. Even if the court orders restitution in such cases, it might well be a meaningless gesture as far as the victim is concerned.

Homeowners insurance and special loss policies cover loss by theft or vandalism, and it is certainly in your interest to be protected this way. You must deal with your insurance company after a burglary to determine the amount you will be paid, and you must also furnish proof to show you owned the missing items. Sales receipts or photos are particularly helpful to your case. Another good idea is an itemized list of all items of value in your home. While composing such a list may appear a tedious task, its existence and the time and frustration it will save you in the event of a burglary are more than worth the effort expended. Be certain when you purchase an insurance policy that you understand its terms and have thoroughly considered adding riders to the policy to cover special valuables. John Jones wished he'd paid more attention when he signed his policy.

John owned a special Oriental carpet valued at $5,000. One night it was rolled up and taken out of his house by a burglar. John was annoyed the next day to learn that his policy limited payment for such special items to a maximum of $1,000. Many policies place such limitations on valuables, including jewelry.

Whether your insurance company will give you a payment equal to the missing item's actual value or to its replacement value may also be an issue. The stereo you purchased three years ago may cost twice as much to replace today. Check your policy, and be aware of your options.

If you are unable to obtain restitution from the defendant or your insurance company, you may still be able to deduct your loss as a casualty loss on your income tax. How much financial relief this step will provide depends on your tax bracket. Another option is to determine whether the negligence of a third party may have been responsible for your loss.

On the day Todd and Sue moved into their new apartment they told the landlord that the lock on their door was flimsy and easily opened. The landlord promised to repair it immediately. Two days went by without the repair. Todd and Sue complained, and the landlord once again assured them that he would take care of the lock.

That very evening while Todd and Sue were out shopping their apartment was burglarized. The couple held the landlord responsible for their loss because they had notified him of the defective lock and he had assumed the obligation to repair it. In this case the intruder was

not caught and the tenants had not yet purchased renters'
insurance. The landlord was found negligent, and Todd
and Sue successfully recovered in court all of their loss.

To recover losses sustained in burglaries

- you must be able to prove your loss with photographs or receipts
- you may receive restitution from the defendant by
  order of the court
- you may be reimbursed by your insurance company
- you may be able to deduct your loss from your
  income tax
- you may be reimbursed by third parties whose negligence may be found responsible for the crime

Additional Problems

Stolen items that have been recovered and items that have
been taken from your house by the police as evidence
are sometimes difficult to retrieve. Their return frequently
depends on your persistence.

It is not uncommon for a stolen ten-speed bike to be
recovered by the police. When an arrest is made, a police
officer may tell the owner that the bicycle must be held
for evidence until the trial of the defendant, a period that
could be six to eight months. However, holding a bicycle
or other item as evidence is not always required; there
are provisions that allow a court to photograph the item
and then return it to its rightful owner.

The same is true of tires taken from an automobile.

Obviously, the automobile is inoperable without them. If the tires were held as evidence, in effect, the owner would be victimized twice. Here again, persistence can make possible special arrangements for the return of the tires through the district attorney handling the case.

There are other problems that crop up as a result of a burglary. Credit cards, blank checks, personal notes, prescriptions, or other items that you didn't notice right away may be missing. First, attempt to determine the extent of your property before the burglary occurred. Notify any companies involved of missing credit cards, and your banks of missing blank checks or savings passbooks. They will advise you about ways to protect yourself from additional theft. Resolve to take photographs of your property routinely each year so that you will know and can prove what you have in your possession. Resolve to keep a separate list of credit cards and a record of your checking and savings accounts.

The best way to deal with burglaries is to prevent them. Secure your property, use common sense, develop a neighborhood watch system. Some people install burglar alarms and others obtain guard dogs as pets. Many homeowners leave their homes in the care of house sitters when they go on vacation. All these measures reduce the risk of burglary.

LARCENY-THEFT

David Whitaker parked his new foreign car overnight in front of his home. The next morning all four of his hub-

caps were missing. His new camera outfit, which had been inadvertently left on the back seat, was also gone.

The unlawful taking of property from the possession of another person is a larceny-theft. This type of crime includes thefts of property from motor vehicles, thefts of motor vehicle parts and accessories, shoplifting, pocket picking, purse snatching, and automobile and bicycle thefts. In all these cases there is no use of force or violence.

In 1981, nearly 7.2 million larceny-thefts were reported to the police. Countless other cases go unreported because the victims believe nothing can be done. Some individuals are motivated to report such incidents because they want to catch the thief or because they want a police report for insurance or income tax purposes.

Only 19 percent of larceny-thefts reported are actually cleared and only a portion of those result in arrest. More than one-third of all reported larceny-thefts involve the theft of automobiles, auto parts, or items left inside automobiles.

Prevention is the best way to combat this crime. Manufacturers have attempted to lower the rate of theft of auto parts by providing inside hood latches, special recessed door locks, and security covers to conceal items placed in the vehicle. Lock any items you wish to secure in your automobile in the trunk. When parking your automobile at night, find a well-lighted space or a parking garage with an attendant.

If you become the victim of a larceny-theft, report it to the police. This is the first step toward recovering your

property. You will also be helping the police determine
if a crime pattern exists. If so, authorities can implement
a prevention program.

In some cities the police will not send an officer to
see you to take a larceny-theft report involving a small
amount. You may have to fill out a form yourself and
mail it to the police department. Larceny-thefts get low
priority from the police, who must concentrate on more
serious crimes.

David Whitaker was lucky. He reported his hubcaps
and camera stolen. His camera was recovered, after the
thief tried to sell it to Bill Wright, a camera dealer. Wright
noted the initials, D.W., and a series of numbers etched
on the camera with an electric pencil. Leery of people
wishing to sell him equipment, Wright contacted the police, who readily recognized the number as a driver's
license number. An officer checked the number on the
state license computer and traced the camera's ownership
to David Whitaker. The thief was arrested after David
positively identified the camera.

David requested his expensive camera be returned to
him pending trial. Special arrangements were made
through the district attorney's office to permit return of
the camera. If David had not made the request, he might
have been without his camera for several months.

David Whitaker was wise in having his camera marked
with his identification. The police often recover stolen
property but cannot determine the rightful owner, so any
valuable personal property should be marked with permanent identification. Your police department can offer
advice and assist you in marking your valuables. Police

technicians will show you how to etch your driver's license number, social security number, or other identification on television sets, stereos, and various personal items. These measures will ensure return of a stolen item and may dissuade a thief from taking it in the first place.

Unfortunately for David, the thief denied any knowledge of the missing hubcaps. They were gone forever.

Bicycle Thefts

More than 650,000 bicycle thefts were reported in 1981. The popular ten-speed bike, which has an average value of $275, is easy to steal and is often taken for a joy ride. Many of them, though recovered by police, are never returned because bikes lack identification. Mark your name on your bike and use a hardened cable to secure it to a guard rail, tree, post, or other heavy, stationary object, measures that may discourage and prevent thefts.

Stolen Motor Vehicles

More than three-quarters of the 1,073,988 vehicles reported stolen in 1981 were automobiles. That they can be repainted quickly and their identifications easily changed means they can be sold rapidly. For these and other reasons only 14 percent of all stolen motor vehicle cases in this country are solved.

If you have a comprehensive automobile insurance policy, most of your loss will be covered by insurance. You may not be paid the full amount you believe your car is worth because in calculating payment, the insurance company considers the *average value* of similar automobiles. An additional problem when your automobile is stolen is the possible loss of any items in it at the time of the theft. When that happens, you can only hope your car has merely been driven around town by the thief and then abandoned.

Recently an upstate New York doctor's automobile was stolen. His only copy of two years of cancer research reports was in the trunk. The police made his case a priority and were able to locate his late-model car several miles away from where it was taken. The doctor, however, has learned to keep extra copies of his reports.

Credit Card Thefts

Few people carry cash when they plan to purchase expensive items. Credit cards and checks are more common. Businesses, however, must protect themselves against fraudulent use of credit cards, so they often require that purchases by credit card for more than $50 be approved by phone. If you have lost a credit card or it has been stolen, report it immediately to the credit card company so that no further purchases are approved. Taking this step limits your liability.

Bad Checks

Sometimes checks you accept from individuals are no good. There may be insufficient funds in the person's

account to cover the check; the account may be closed
or nonexistent, or the person giving you the check may
have forged another person's name. In any of these instances you lose the money that you were promised by
the check.

Both police and the courts place collection of a bad
check as a very low priority in the criminal justice system.
In special circumstances, you may press the police and
district attorney to arrest and prosecute a person for issuing a bad check. However, you may be required to file
the accusatory instrument yourself.

Often, if left to his own initiative, a district attorney
will prosecute a person on bad check charges only if he
has committed the violation several times. In such instances your chances of restitution are minimal.

If you persist in having a person arrested and prosecuted on bad check charges, be prepared to follow through.
Don't consider it a simple way to obtain restitution. You
will have to be available for hearings or a trial.

To prevent such a loss, be careful when accepting
checks. Looking at a person's driver's license or other
identification does not ensure that an account exists or
that there is money in the bank; it only assists you in
determining the identity of the person writing the check.
If you have any questions about the value of a check,
insist that it be certified or contact the bank where the
check is to be negotiated. If it's permitted, request that
a hold be placed on the check writer's funds. Many people
are merely poor bookkeepers and do not intentionally
write bad checks. When this happens no violation of

criminal law occurs, for the intent to defraud *must* be demonstrated.

VANDALISM

One evening Bill and Jeff walked casually down a residential street in their neighborhood. They took turns with Jeff's new BB gun, shooting out light bulbs in the old-fashioned light posts illuminating the neighborhood. An alert neighbor called the police, who responded quickly, and the two vandals' spree was soon ended.

After appearing in local court, Bill and Jeff were ordered to pay for the damage. They also were sentenced to work forty hours on the grounds of a local park.

A few of the common types of vandalism involve broken windows, paint sprayed on houses and cars, snapped antennas, and damaged mailboxes. Vandalism usually occurs at night and usually the culprits are not caught.

Vandalism, the reckless or intentional damage to property, is classified as criminal mischief. Nearly everyone is affected by it at some time. It is an impersonal act, but it is annoying and destructive. It is frequently a result of teenagers showing off or expressing anger. Neither they nor other vandals stop to consider the results of their actions.

It has been demonstrated, however, that young people who are apprehended and made to account for their actions are less likely to repeat such acts. In view of this, many judges and police youth officers have adopted a policy of requiring swift action by the vandal to right the wrong that was committed. Many authorities seek to tailor the punishment to fit the violation.

For example, Bruce spray-painted a house. The court ordered him to restore the house to its original condition and also to devote thirty hours in helping to paint a public building.

In another case Tom smashed the picture window in a house owned by a man he did not like. He had to compensate his victim by cutting his lawn free of charge all summer. Such punishments instill a sense of accountability. The victims are usually happy that actual work is accomplished.

But many vandals are not caught and made accountable for their acts and misdeeds. Often the path of their destruction is not discovered until much later. To discourage vandalism, you can set up neighborhood watch programs and request that police increase their patrols in the area. Better night lighting is also an effective measure.

Some communities and states have passed ordinances placing responsibility on parents or guardians for damage done by their children. In some communities youth peer jury programs have been effective in reducing vandalism.

If you are a victim of a vandal, report the incident to the police and get an accurate estimate of the repair. Be sure the authorities know you want to be compensated for your loss if a person is arrested. Find out if your insurance covers vandalism claims. Many policies have deductible provisions that effectively exclude vandalism claims. You can take a deduction on your income tax for a casualty loss if you have not been otherwise compensated.

To combat criminal mischief

- report all incidents of damage
- get neighbors involved in a neighborhood watch program
- insist that your community make vandals accountable
- improve lighting in high vandalism areas
- check your insurance coverage
- find out if you can take a tax deduction for casualty loss
- work to pass ordinances making parents or guardians accountable for misdeeds of youths
- seek to have the punishment fit the violation

The probability of solving crimes of vandalism—as well as burglary and larceny-thefts—is relatively low. Your best efforts should be directed to the prevention of these crimes. In the event of such a crime, report it and follow through until you reach a satisfactory resolution. If the case has a low priority with you, you can be sure it will have a low priority in the criminal justice system.

CHAPTER 9

CRIMES COMMITTED IN THE USE OF A MOTOR VEHICLE

DRIVING WHILE INTOXICATED

Terry and Scott, 7- and 8-year-old brothers, were walking along the shoulder of a highway. They had just spent an afternoon fishing at a nearby creek and were heading home for dinner.

After playing eighteen holes of golf earlier that same afternoon, Sam Spike spent three hours in the clubhouse drinking several extra-dry martinis. A mile from the golf course, Spike, who was unable to drive his car within the lane markers, swerved to the right and hit Scott from behind, hurling the little boy several feet. Terry ran to his brother's lifeless body, which was lying in a pool of blood next to a crumpled guard rail.

Bill Hanson worked overtime as often as possible to earn money for a larger home for his growing family. One night, as he carefully rounded a curve on his way home from work, he saw headlights moving rapidly and directly toward him. The headlights belonged to an out-of-control automobile driven by a 17-year-old who had celebrated the last day of school by drinking all day with four friends. Bill had no chance to avoid the oncoming car. He survived the crash, but his injuries were permanent and disabling.

Susan Lisson had the green light at an intersection not far from the store where she had just purchased her weekly supply of groceries. Her car was hit broadside by another car moving at 50 miles per hour through a red light. Susan died instantly. The driver of the other vehicle had twice before been arrested for driving while intoxicated. He was a confirmed alcoholic, and he continued to drive even though his license had been suspended.

Cases such as these are repeated thousands of times each year. In 1981 there were more than 52,000 deaths on the country's highways. A contributing factor in more than half the deaths was the consumption of alcohol by at least one driver in each collision. In the last decade intoxicated drivers have accounted for five times the number of deaths suffered by the United States during the entire Vietnam War. Each year some 760,000 persons are injured in accidents caused by drunken drivers, and each year the property damage caused by such drivers amounts to nearly $1.5 billion.

How Much Is Legally Drunk

The amount of alcohol in the bloodstream that classifies a person as legally "too drunk to drive" has been reduced over the years. Formerly .15 of 1 percent of alcohol by weight in the bloodstream, the legal limit is now .10 of 1 percent. Some states have set the legal limit even lower.

It takes four to five 12-ounce beers or four to five shots of an 86-proof alcoholic beverage absorbed into the bloodstream to bring the average person's blood alcohol level to the "legally drunk" threshold of .10. A drinker passes one drink per hour through his system, so a person drinking over a three- or four-hour period could actually have as many as nine drinks before being considered legally too drunk to drive. Most persons arrested for driving while intoxicated (DWI) have consumed much more than the legal limit. In the average drunken driver, the alcohol level hovers near the .20 mark.

A person can be charged and convicted even if a test is not taken. If the defendant is unconscious or if the defendant refuses, it may be impossible for the police to give a test. In such cases, trial testimony is based on an officer's experience in judging whether a person is intoxicated. Penalties for drunken driving include suspension or revocation of a driver's license, fines up to $1,000, jail sentences, probation, and a criminal record.

A driver is classified as legally intoxicated by

* the measurement of more than .10 of 1 percent of alcohol by weight in the bloodstream

- the educated judgment of a police officer when the driver refuses, or is unable, to take the blood alcohol test

The Arrest of the Drunken Driver

The potential for death or injury from drinking and driving is more than alarming. Traffic safety officials estimate that on any weekend night one driver out of every ten on the highway is legally drunk. Nationwide, police agencies last year arrested more than 1 million persons for DWI.

Most persons arrested for DWI are stopped before they are involved in a collision with a person, vehicle, or stationary object, thus drivers like Norm Wing are prevented from causing injury or death.

Friday after work is happy hour for Norm Wing. One Friday at 5 P.M. he went to a favorite downtown bar to take advantage of the two-for-one specials. Several drinks and three hours later, he wound his way to a disco in his suburban town, where he had several more drinks. At midnight Wing got into his car and headed home. A mile from the disco a police officer noticed Wing's slow-moving car straddling the center line. The car had no lights.

Officer Eugene Shaw believed he had cause to stop a drunken driver, so he signaled Wing's vehicle to the side of the road and asked to see Wing's driver's license. After much difficulty and fumbling, Wing found his license and handed it to the officer.

Shaw detected the strong smell of alcohol on Wing's breath. Then he turned his light on Wing's face. It revealed bloodshot eyes. Wing's words were slow and slurred.

The officer asked Wing to get out of his car and perform some tests: walking, heel to toe, touching his nose, and reciting the alphabet. His performance in all instances was poor. He was placed under arrest for driving while intoxicated and put in the back seat of Shaw's patrol vehicle. Wing was taken to the local police station after his car was towed away.

After being advised of his constitutional rights and his right to take a test to determine the alcohol in his bloodstream, Wing consented to take a blood alcohol test. The result was .17. Wing, who had never been arrested before, was released to the custody of a friend, who assured police that she would drive him directly home.

To stop a vehicle, a police officer must have cause to believe a person is drunk. Any traffic violation—speeding, going through a red light, driving too slowly, driving on the wrong side of the road, failing to yield the right of way, illegal license plates, or an improper inspection certificate—gives an officer probable cause to stop a vehicle. An automobile accident, of course, also forms the basis on which a police officer can begin an investigation.

The officer may observe a driver with a smell of alcohol on his breath who is unable to walk straight, has trouble with balance, has bloodshot eyes and perhaps a disheveled appearance, slurs words, or is generally uncomprehending. The officer may make such observations during a blood alcohol test or independently of a test. If the officer concludes that a person is driving while intoxicated, the person will be arrested and placed in a patrol car; his vehicle will be towed. At the police station the defendant would be given a blood alcohol test, which utilizes a machine called a breathalyzer.

A breathalyzer measures the amount of alcohol by weight in the blood. The person being tested breathes deeply and exhales into a tube connected to the machine. This exhaled air is then analyzed chemically in a matter of seconds. The accuracy of breathalyzer tests has been upheld in the courts.

Alternative tests include chemical analyses of the urine or blood. The breath test is most commonly used and is preferred by police because results are available immediately.

Defendants Have Many Rights

Most states classify DWI as a crime. An arrest must be based on probable cause.

A person charged with DWI is entitled, just as any other defendant, to bail and release. Often police officers permit a friend or relative to take the defendant home. A court date for arraignment is assigned. Many weeks or months may pass before the case is actually concluded. Police are held to the same high legal standard in DWI cases as they are in any other case.

The test to determine alcohol in the blood must be taken voluntarily by the defendant and must be administered in conformance with very strict standards. Statements made by a DWI defendant at the time of the arrest may be used in court only if the driver was given his or her rights, understood them, and subsequently waived them.

A person charged with DWI is entitled to an attorney, must be brought before a judge, and may demand a trial by jury. The court process becomes lengthy, involved, and time consuming. The case must be proved beyond a reasonable doubt because the presumption of innocence remains until the defendant pleads guilty or is convicted. The whole court process may be prolonged for a period of many months because of the volume of DWI cases.

Unless some particular circumstance causes the judge or district attorney to give a case special attention, DWI cases are treated routinely. For a first violation, the sentence may be a suspension of license or a fine. In some areas first-time offenders are assigned to a rehabilitation or education program. The defendant often continues to drive during the time the case is wending its way through the system.

Most state motor vehicle departments will not suspend a license until a criminal charge has been resolved. In some states the motor vehicle department will revoke a defendant's driving privilege pending an administrative hearing if the person refused to take a blood alcohol test.

In some states, legislation has been passed requiring judges to take the operator's license if the offender has a prior DWI conviction. The Department of Motor Vehicles will then hold a hearing to determine whether to continue holding the license.

Although many licenses are revoked or suspended, some drivers choose to drive anyway. This was the case when eight people were killed near Sacramento, California, by a man who drank too much at a wedding reception and then rammed his car into the back of two automobiles at 90 miles per hour. Although he had been arrested three times previously for DWI, he chose to drive even though his license was revoked. Finally he was sentenced to spend time in the state prison, but the chance that he will repeat his drinking and driving pattern when he gets out remains.

Some states provide mandatory alcohol counseling for any person convicted of an alcohol-related driving offense. This step is effective but costly. Communities must be willing to bear such an expense. Many localities are now imposing mandatory fines, which they apply to rehabilitation programs; the violator, therefore, pays the bill for his own rehabilitation.

Drivers accused of intoxication have the right

- to be stopped only for probable cause
- to bail and release from custody pending trial
- to refuse to take the alcohol blood test
- to an attorney and trial before a judge or jury
- to retain their drivers' licenses pending trial
- to protection from any statements they made at the time of arrest unless it is determined that they understood and waived their constitutional rights in making such statements

THE VICTIMS OF
DRUNKEN DRIVERS

Many people who drink and drive get to their destination without incident. The Norm Wings of this country are stopped by alert police officers. But thousands of others who are less fortunate are responsible for the deaths of many or a lifetime of heartache for innocent victims.

The persons who are plucked from the flow of everyday life to become victims of drunken drivers are guilty of only being in the wrong place at the wrong time. Most victims, like 8-year-old Scott, Bill Hanson, and Susan Lisson, were doing nothing more than going about their lives in an orderly, normal manner when, without warning, they were hit.

For the injured and for the families of victims, there is a surfeit of anger, hostility, grief, and alienation. There are the immediate problems—burying the dead, healing the wounded, and repairing property damage—grievous but necessary tasks. The resulting financial loss and emotional distress may go on for months, years, or even a lifetime.

An extraordinary public campaign against drunken driving has spurred legislation designed to "get tough" with drunken drivers. Special federal and state funds have been awarded to communities establishing programs to get the intoxicated driver off the road before there is destruction of life and property.

Victims of drunken drivers have also banded together. Groups such as MADD (Mothers Against Drunken Drivers), RID (Remove Intoxicated Drivers), and SADD (Students Against Drunken Drivers) have become national advocates for tougher legislation and practical programs.

In most areas of the country counseling for victims is provided on a professional and/or peer group level. In many communities local groups have sprung up in reaction to drunken driving, such as RAID (Rochester Against Intoxicated Drivers).

The numerous groups and extensive legislative lobbying have had positive results. Tough new laws have been enacted, community awareness has led to education programs, prosecutors responsible to the community have taken tougher stands, and plea bargaining has been reduced and in some areas even eliminated. Significantly, the president of the United States has empowered a national commission to attack the problem of drunken driving.

An intoxicated driver who causes the death of another person can be charged by the district attorney with a felony of manslaughter or criminal negligent homicide. If there is no death but there is serious injury, a felony assault may be charged. The drunken driver's actions place him or her in the same class as a violent criminal; instead of a gun or a knife, the weapons are alcohol and an automobile.

Victims in the Court System

In spite of the problems that often hang heavy on their lives, most victims of drunken drivers want to see justice done. They may want the defendant's license taken away and swift punishment for his or her actions. Often, the day after the defendant is arrested for DWI, he or she simply shows up at the police department to pay the towing bill on the car and drives away again. Victims have a right to ask, "What will happen tonight? Will this person drink again and cause another accident?"

Victims have a right to be informed. They are entitled to and should receive information, but as has been pointed out in earlier chapters, prosecutors rarely contact victims. Again, the large volume of cases they must handle usually prevents them from doing so. If you're a victim, take the initiative. Find out which district attorney is in charge of the case. Contact that person by phone and make him or her aware of your interest in the case. Say you want to have some input in the case and that you are willing to testify at any time. Follow up your conversation with a letter. If you do not hear further, check again in a few weeks. If you are not satisfied with the response you receive, contact the chief district attorney, your elected official. Elected officials are very sensitive about serving you and giving you information to which you are entitled.

Your persistence will produce results. The prosecutor will make sure your case is handled personally. Your wishes will be considered by the prosecutor and heard by the judge. If your concern is to get the defendant off the road, make sure these people know it. If you believe an alcohol rehabilitation program would be beneficial or that jail would be more appropriate, say so. Follow Carol Russo's example.

Although no one was hurt when Mike Paul crashed into her car, Carol Russo soon learned that the $436 in damages was not covered by Paul's insurance. After Paul was arrested on a DWI charge, Carol called the district attorney handling the case and told him she wanted restitution. She sent an estimate of repairs to the judge and a copy of her letter to the district attorney. In disposing of the case, the judge ordered that, before anything else, Carol Russo be paid in full. You should follow the same procedure if your property is damaged by a DWI defendant. If you collect under your own insurance, you may still have a deductible of $100 or $500 that can be covered by the defendant. Take care of such a matter as soon as you can so that the court may assist you in obtaining payment if necessary.

Victims of DWI defendants should

- contact the district attorney in charge of the case by phone and letter
- notify the district attorney that they are willing to testify and advise him or her of their phone numbers both at work and at home
- ask the district attorney to keep them posted on the progress of the case
- call the district attorney for updates
- tell the district attorney that they are interested in getting the driver off the road, obtaining restitution, getting rehabilitation for the driver, and sentencing the driver to either jail or work in the community

- obtain repair estimates and submit them to the district attorney and the judge

Civil Remedies

The victim of a drunken driver also has the right to sue to collect civil damages. If you are injured, you may bring action for reimbursement of your medical bills and compensation for pain, suffering, injuries, and lost wages. Awards have ranged from a few hundred dollars into the millions. If your disability has left you unable to work and you are supporting a family—as was the case with Bill Hanson—the value of your damages would be great. To bring a civil action, you must consult an attorney, who will advise you about how to proceed and how to handle your case.

In the event of death, family members may bring an action for their loss. The amount sought varies greatly, depending on who and how many persons depended financially on the person killed, as well as the earning power of the deceased. Reimbursement for burial expenses can be sought.

The death of a parent, husband, or wife is considered a greater financial loss than the death of a child. The financial value of civil litigation is highest when the family breadwinner loses his or her life.

Civil cases for compensation are not prosecuted by the district attorney but are handled by your own personal attorney. Any award or settlement obtained is usually paid by the drunken driver's insurance. In Sid Jones' case, however, as in many other cases, such insurance was insufficient.

Sid Jones, the victim of a drunken driver, was out of work for nearly one year. In addition to his pain and suffering, he was permanently blinded in one eye. He sued, and the jury awarded $475,000. The driver's insurance covered only $100,000. Sid then looked to alternative sources for compensation. Because his own automobile insurance provided coverage for under-insured motorists, he was able to obtain an additional $100,000. To obtain the balance, he filed a judgment against the driver, which placed a lien against the defendant's home and future wages. Other options included foreclosing on the defendant's real property and garnisheeing his wages.

In addition to a civil action against a drunken driver, a victim may also sue the person who may have contributed to the driver's drunkenness. A bar owner continued to serve a customer even though it was apparent that the customer was intoxicated. The bartender subsequently was held responsible and ordered to pay $125,000 to a victim in a third-party action. Third-party actions have become more common as courts place responsibility for excessive drinking on those who benefit from the sale of intoxicating beverages.

Of course, there are convicted drunken drivers who have neither insurance nor assets. However, if a court makes an award in a civil case, the victim can still be paid. Victims' compensation boards in most states compensate victims and their families when there is no other source of compensation. The programs in thirty-eight states are described in the Appendix A.

To obtain compensation, a victim may

- seek restitution by direct payment from the defendant
- bring legal action against the defendant that his or her insurance company will indemnify, with any excess becoming a judgment and lien
- bring actions against third parties who contributed to the drunkenness of the defendant
- apply to victims' compensation board

OTHER VEHICLE CRIMES

A person does not have to be intoxicated to commit a crime while driving a vehicle. Take, for instance, the case of a young driver who became angry when he was denied admission to a carnival in a midwestern city. The youth climbed into his car and raced recklessly at a high rate of speed out of the parking lot. As he left, his car struck several persons.

The youth was charged with leaving the scene of an accident and with assault, for causing injury to the pedestrians. Alcohol was not involved, but his conduct showed an indifference to human life; he was charged, appropriately, with reckless endangerment.

Other types of vehicle-related crimes occur when a car or truck is used in place of a weapon to intentionally cause damage to another person. Procedures used in the criminal justice system and remedies available to victims are discussed in Chapter 6.

CHAPTER 10

FAMILY CRIMES

In 1981 more than 4,500 murders were committed within families or by persons who had intimate relationships with their victims. Often, in these relationships, rage had mounted over a long period of time. Our society is built on the sanctity of the family. Many persons believe that life is most complete and rewarding for members of an intact family unit. A victim's fear of destroying this image is often the reason he or she fails to report to authorities crimes among family members.

Spouse abuse, incest, and child abuse and neglect occur in families of all social and economic levels. Actions that would otherwise be criminally prosecuted are tolerated by victims within a family. A wife may fear her husband but not report him because he supports her. She may have been intimidated into believing that she has no right to prosecute her husband. A child may not know that having sexual relations with her brother or stepfather is inappropriate. A relative may not wish to report a mother who beats her young children or leaves them alone for long periods of time. Some people convince themselves that they can tolerate a tragic situation or that a family should resolve its own problems.

Family members have the same rights as if the acts committed against them were perpetrated by strangers. Recently the criminal justice system has developed new sensitivity toward the plight of the victim of domestic violence, incest, and child abuse and neglect.

WIFE ABUSE

John and Susan were married four months after she found out she was pregnant. When the child was two years old, Susan became pregnant again. The timing was unfortunate. They lived in a one-bedroom apartment in a run-down neighborhood. John had just lost his low-paying job because the local factory had closed. Bills had piled up, and the future looked bleak. The prospect of having another child troubled both John and Susan. Before their marriage John had "roughed up" Susan occasionally when things hadn't gone well; now he blamed Susan for all his disappointments and for his inability to provide for the family. He began to beat her daily. One night he came home drunk, even more so than usual, and hit Susan very hard several times. She slipped into a semiconscious state. At the hospital, medical personnel called the police.

Kathy and Bill, married for ten years, were parents of three children, aged 7, 6, and 4 years. They lived together in a nicely decorated, upper-middle-class home. Just after their second child was born, Bill started to do strange things at home. He punished his children physically and severely. When Kathy objected, Bill pushed and shoved her, too. Kathy tolerated the situation for many years; she was afraid that telling someone would upset the family and that she would lose everything. With marriage to Bill came a home, jewels, and fine clothes. The community considered Bill and Kathy an ideal couple. The shame and embarrassment she was convinced she would bring to the family by seeking legal action deterred her from taking any action at all.

One day Bill came home from work in a rage and told her he was going to kill her if she didn't stay home all day, every day. He then knocked her down with a single swing of his arm. Kathy's fear of shame and embarrassment evaporated. She called the domestic violence hotline, a division of the county district attorney's office.

Susan and Kathy tolerated abuse too long. If they had refused to accept victimization, they might have been able to save years of anguish for themselves and their families.

Reports to authorities of family violence come from hospital personnel, teachers, family doctors, relatives, friends, and finally, the victims.

Many women are simply too terrified to call the police or someone else for help. Nan felt like a prisoner in her home. Her husband, Dick, monitored every move she made. If she went out of the house without his permission, she was punished severely. She feared that if she called the police and they *didn't* take him away she would be severely beaten. One day she saw on television a public service announcement for a group called Alternatives for Battered Women. She quickly jotted down the phone number. It took her two days to muster the courage to call the group's telephone hotline. After describing her plight to the counselor over the phone, she learned that emergency housing was available in a secure area for both herself and her children for a period of up to thirty days. During this time she would receive counseling to help her deal with her problem.

In your own area there are organizations whose purpose it is, among others, to advise victims of domestic abuse of their rights. Groups such as Alternatives for Battered Women and family crisis centers provide crisis counseling for women and information on how to deal with victimization. All options, including arrest, are explained. Many communities provide shelter for a short period of time so that a woman and her children can escape the rage of an abusive husband and father. Many police agencies and district attorney offices provide domestic violence bureaus staffed by trained personnel to inform victims of their rights within the legal system.

· What to Do If You Are the Victim of a Wife Beater

Susan and Kathy did not know that they had alternatives to the threats, fear, and violence in their lives. If you are a victim of domestic violence, it is important that you decide upon your ultimate goal. Ask yourself these questions: *Do I want to try to save my family relationship and go through counseling? Do I feel that my unhappiness would be over if I were separated from my husband?* You must develop a plan based on your answers. Your local counselor may assist you.

One option, and a swift one, is to have your husband arrested if he has threatened you or caused you physical injury. To obtain the best results, call the police at the time of the incident. A police officer will protect your safety and evaluate the problem. If it is clear that violence has just taken place or if it occurs in the presence of a police officer, he can physically arrest your husband and remove him from your home at your request. If the turmoil has subsided or your report is delayed, you will have to file the charges yourself. Go to the local criminal court office to get an arrest warrant. You must document the incident and be prepared to prove your injuries. Provide court officials with names of witnesses, photographs of your bruises, and any medical records of your injuries.

An arrest may stop the violence or shock your husband so that he agrees to work with you toward a better future. He is now, for the first time, being held accountable for his actions by an authoritative figure. If being together is no longer possible, your action may establish the ground rules for your new life apart.

When your husband is arrested, he may be held in custody until the next session of court. You should appear at that session and tell the district attorney what results you wish to achieve. The district attorney, who acts as your attorney in a criminal action, will advise you of the options available.

You may obtain an order of protection, an injunction designed to prevent violence by one member of a household against another. This is a written document, signed by the judge, that orders your husband to stop threatening you or hitting you. It may direct him to leave the house and stay away from you and your children for a period of time. The judge may set any other conditions he believes necessary for your safety. If your husband disobeys an order of protection, a police officer has the authority to lock him up until he again appears before the judge. While the case is pending, the judge may also order you and your husband to participate in certain domestic violence prevention programs.

And there are other options for you and the court. If there is a conviction, a permanent order of protection may be granted; your husband may be placed on probation; or, in extreme cases of violence, a jail sentence may be imposed.

If you fail to appear at the initial court appearance, however, these results will not be possible. Furthermore, the next time you call the police, although they will act to prevent violence, they may not be as eager to assist you in the court process.

At the first court appearance the case is scheduled for a second court date for which your husband must return. You, too, should appear at the next and all other court sessions to express your desires to the judge and the district attorney.

If you have your husband arrested, be prepared to

- document your claim with witnesses, photographs, police reports, or other evidence
- follow through on your plan to obtain results
- keep the district attorney aware of your wishes
- appear at each court date
- be consistent in your plan once you have implemented it

As a battered wife, you have the option in most states of filing your charge in the local criminal court and having it proceed as an ordinary criminal case. Or, you may file a petition in the domestic relations court in your county, most often known as family court. There are advantages and disadvantages to both options. Both courts may order your husband to move out of your house and stay away from you for a time until your relationship is resolved. Both courts can issue orders and protections if good cause is shown. However, family court may not be the speediest procedure because it only meets during the day and in special sessions. Local criminal court, on the other hand, is swift in initial action, but cases tend to get lost in the shuffle afterwards. Officials in your community can advise you of the best court to use in your particular case.

In either court there's an alternative to a trial and full prosecution. Your case may be assigned to a diversion program, which provides counseling and possibly referrals for your own housing, legal services, and/or the introduction of child abuse prevention programs. Ultimately you will have to resolve your future in a face-to-face discussion with your husband. To achieve this end you may be sent to your local center for dispute settlement or to another arbitration program that often exists as part of the district attorney's domestic violence bureau.

Susan, Kathy, and Nan all took different routes to break out of the battered spouse syndrome. Communities are now well equipped to assist you in dealing head on with this problem. As a victim, it is imperative that you take action and be prepared to follow through at every stage to achieve a result that could save you and your family from further anguish—and injury.

As the victim of a wife beater you can

- call the police and have your husband arrested
- obtain court-ordered counseling for your husband and your family
- obtain an order of protection
- decide after counseling to keep the family together
. or to separate

HUSBANDS ARE BATTERED, TOO

Much of the discussion here has dealt with women who have been assaulted and abused by their husbands. Yet many husbands are physically abused and harassed by their spouses. Men are not as "trapped" as women, and society permits them to take action with much more ease

than their wives. There are, however, groups to assist
men who are battered. All of the rights and actions available to women are as readily available to men.

CHILD ABUSE

*Frank and June never could agree on the proper way to
teach and discipline their two sons. Frank demanded
instant compliance to a direction from the time each child
was old enough to walk. If the child did not respond to
direction instantly, Frank took off his belt and hit a nearby
object. Frequently, when a child did not scurry fast
enough, the belt would strike him. For the supreme punishment, Frank ordered the child to take off his shirt and
then hit him on the back with the belt. Frank posted a
schedule of punishment, listing the number of strikes he
had assigned each violation. When the older son, Billy,
was a second grader, his torment was discovered during
a routine school physical examination. The school doctor
immediately contacted the County Department of Social
Services, and the child protective division conducted an
investigation.*

Child abuse takes many forms. The physical abuse Frank
meted out to his children was the result of the punishment
his own father had used on him. Because of his upbring-
ing, he was unable to communicate in an understanding
way with his children. He was, however, a good provider
for his family and otherwise cared for them.

After receiving the report on Billy's injuries, a child

protective worker contacted the family and conducted an investigation to see if charges should be brought. Frank's response to the protective worker showed his lack of understanding. He felt his punishments fit the children's actions. Nobody was going to tell him how to bring up his kids. The protective worker brought charges in family court against Frank for child abuse. Frank was notified to appear in court within a few days.

A judge in such a case has many options. He or she can order a child removed from the home and placed with a foster family until he or she decides it is safe for the child to return. Or the court can order the father removed from the home and away from the child. In Frank's case, both these remedies appeared too drastic. Instead, the court issued an order of protection, which directed Frank to keep his hands away from the children and his belt secured to his pants. Frank was to undergo counseling himself and in sessions with his family. During this time the child protective service worker would make periodic visits to the home.

That Frank's father had used the same discipline for him was uncovered in counseling; Frank did not know any other method. Over a three-month period he was taught how to deal with his anger. He also learned new and acceptable methods of disciplining his boys. The chain of abuse that had been passed on to him by his father had been broken. Frank acknowledged to the judge that he felt much better about himself in learning how to deal with his children.

His son Billy also went through counseling with his father so that he could understand why his father had acted out anger in such an awful way. Billy learned how to defuse his own hostilities so that he could function well with others and so that he wouldn't pass on this violence to his own children.

CHILD NEGLECT

Sara, a single parent, worked all day and left her children, aged 4 and 7, with her sister when they weren't in school. On several evenings each week she left home to socialize after the children were asleep, believing that if the youngsters were asleep no harm could come to them. A neighbor who was upset with this arrangement notified authorities.

Neglect is another form of child abuse. It occurs when a parent leaves children alone and unsupervised. There may be no apparent physical harm.

Suzanne was brought into family court on a child neglect petition for bringing her 6- and 8-year-old daughters into a bar while she partied one night. The judge ordered her not to take the children into the bar again. One month later a police officer passing Suzanne's usual hangout spotted her car parked in front. Her two children, dressed only in light clothes despite freezing temperatures, were seated in the car. The officer learned that Suzanne had been told not to bring the children into the bar and that her method of obeying was to leave them alone in the car.

   An investigation was conducted and the child protection worker recommended to the judge that the children be placed in foster care until Suzanne could demonstrate responsibility in caring for them. In this case, therapy and education took a very long time.

The victims of child abuse and neglect become resigned to abuse and neglect as a way of life. Many of these children grow up to be hostile, angry adults who mete out their anger on their own children and/or society. However, groups such as Parents Anonymous, Children's Alliance, and others have been established nationwide. They stand ready to assist victims and their parents in their efforts to discontinue such cycles of neglect.

Reporting child abuse and neglect is the responsibility of everyone in the community. As a neighbor, friend, or relative, you can anonymously report a case to child protective services, the district attorney, or the police. In some areas toll-free hotlines exist for anonymous reports. These reports are followed by swift investigation.

The law in most states requires doctors, nurses, teachers, counselors, social workers, and day-care workers to report actual or suspected cases of child abuse and neglect; failure to act can be punishable by a fine.

SEXUAL ABUSE AND INCEST

Sexual abuse and incest practiced among family members can be the most desperate and horrid of family crimes. *Any sexual contact between an adult and child is considered sexual abuse.*

Sexual abuse can be assaultive in nature, such as rape or sodomy committed on a child, or non-assaultive, such as fondling incidents.

Although young girls are usually the victims, boys are involved in about 25 percent of all reported cases. Unfortunately, most cases of sexual abuse are not reported. A young girl may feel that this sexual activity is a necessary part of being loved and accepted; she may not realize that the relationship is improper until she starts talking with other girls her age who have healthy family lives. She may then become upset, enraged, and feel trapped.

Stephen married Annie's mother when Annie was 3 years old. Soon after the marriage, Annie sought, as many children do, the warmth of her mother and stepfather's bed. As time went on, Stephen began to hug, clutch, and fondle Annie. By the time she was 10 years old this activity had evolved into more intimate sexual contact and occurred only when Stephen and Annie were alone. When Annie reached puberty, she began discussing her sexual knowledge with friends. One of her playmates told her own mother about Annie's comments, and the playmate's mother notified the county child protective service. Within days, Stephen was arrested for endangering the welfare of a child. He refused to acknowledge that his was a wrong act and insisted that he was expressing his love in "a European way" for his stepdaughter. Eventually he was jailed for a period of time.

As with Stephen and Annie, most sexual abuse cases within the family involve girls between the ages of 10 and 15 and their stepfathers. The community must be made aware of the need to take swift action in such circumstances, and children should be taught, even at a

young age, the difference between normal and abnormal
expressions of affection.

Victims of child abuse can be helped by

- the anonymous reporting of suspected cases
- the prosecution of the abuser in family court
- a court order of protection
- the community groups dedicated to the elimination
  of child abuse
- the passage of laws requiring the reporting of such
  abuses

Victims of family crimes should speak out and end their
torment. Communities must realize that this victimization
affects everyone. Each citizen has an obligation to report
incidents of abuse and stand by to give ready assistance
within the system. Crime should not be permitted to draw
a veil of secrecy around a family.

CHAPTER 11

VICTIMLESS CRIMES

Not all offenses regarded as violations of criminal law are of great concern to all members of the community. When a victim suffers physical injury or incurs monetary loss, there is a public cry for arrest, prosecution, and accountability. Less public concern is shown for cases involving prostitution and gambling, however, because all the participants appear to be willingly involved and safe from physical harm. The general belief is that police, prosecutors, judges, and other public officials should not be concerned with such crimes. Doesn't it make more sense, the public often asks, to spend valuable law enforcement time trying to solve and prosecute real crime? The public is too often naive, or has misconceptions, about the so-called victimless crimes.

There are no *victimless* crimes. Prostitution and illegal gambling networks create victims.

PROSTITUTION

George had yet another fight with his wife over family finances. In a huff, he left home late on a Friday night, and drove to a boulevard where he knew companionship was available. As he slowly cruised in his van, scantily clad girls waved at him from the sidewalks. He stopped for a brief conversation, then let two of them get into his van. They had each agreed to perform sexual acts with him for $20. George thought the price was a bargain. Several hours later his van was found parked at the end of a darkened street, his lifeless body slumped across the front seat. He had been stabbed in the heart three times. His jewelry and wallet were gone, and the inside of his van had been stripped.

Barbara had had many disagreements with her parents, and she was clearly becoming more and more difficult to handle. At age 15, she took the money she had saved and bought a bus ticket to a large city in her home state. She had little idea of what she was going to do when she got there; she just knew she had to get away from her parents' authority and be on her own.

Fear and loneliness mixed with the noise and excitement of the dazzling city. Soon Barbara was without money and a place to sleep. She became acquainted with some other girls who had been in the city for months, and they taught her the way of the streets. Within a few days she found how easy it was to stand on street corners frequented by prostitutes and make her own deals. Soon a man named Arthur befriended her. In exchange for

*working for him she received a place to stay, food, and
also drugs—he became her pimp.*

*At first she only had to turn over some of her profits
to Arthur, but it was not long before he gave her quotas
to meet: "Bring in two hundred dollars a night or else!"
Sometimes she brought in even more, which pleased her
pimp. However, when she didn't hand over enough money
she was beaten and accused of holding back funds. In
desperation she added stealing and violence to her role
as a prostitute.*

Both George and Barbara are victims of street prostitution. Their stories are not unusual but very typical of
urban areas in the United States. Not all men known as
"Johns" reach such tragic ends, of course, but the goal
of street prostitutes is to bring home to their pimp as
much cash as he requires in exchange for food, shelter,
attention, and drugs; this is accomplished not only by
turning a trick for $20 but by stealing wallets, jewelry,
or anything else a John may possess. Resistance by the
John is usually met with violence; knives, guns, and pins
are all part of the regular arsenal of the street prostitute.

Street prostitutes know that the possibility of getting
arrested for serious crimes is slim. Most incidents of
thievery and violence by street prostitutes are not reported
to police. It is the rare complainant who wishes to suffer
the embarrassment of reporting that a prostitute was in
his company.

Many prostitutes also cause health problems. They are
carriers of all forms of disease, including venereal disease.

Girls like Barbara—confused, young, and naive—are unknowing victims, prey who become hooked as hookers. Once indebted to a pimp, they find it virtually impossible to break away from him or the cycle in which they're caught. Beatings, drugs, and a life of crime are their plight. They have no escape.

Once New York's 42nd Street, Miami's Biscayne Boulevard, Los Angeles' Sunset Boulevard, and countless other streets were considered points of pride in beautiful and important neighborhoods. Now, however, these famous thoroughfares have given way to the sort of neighborhood disintegration and urban blight that prostitution and all that it brings with it—massage parlors, sex shops, x-rated movie houses, drug dealers—inflict. The neighborhood and its residents are the victims.

The person primarily responsible for victims of street prostitution is the pimp. He uses the weak in society to prey upon the vulnerability of others.

It is usually difficult for police to arrest pimps. The witnesses against them, their girls, are often lulled into a state of security or frightened to such a degree that they would never testify. Many times a prostitute who has suffered a beating so severe that she ends up in the emergency room of a hospital still refuses to name the person who has abused her.

Frustrated by the difficulties involved in obtaining enough evidence to arrest a pimp, police authorities try instead to clean up their communities by arresting prostitutes on the streets; a measure that does have an impact on the pimp's operation—and helps keep the public from using the services of those particular prostitutes.

Often police set up decoy operations in which a female officer poses as a prostitute. In this way, Johns can be arrested for patronizing a prostitute. Not long ago, New York City went so far as to broadcast the names of arrested Johns on the radio, a move intended to dissuade men from the temptation of buying services from a street prostitute because of the humiliation and embarrassment such exposure would inflict on them and their families. However, this became extremely controversial because of the legal rights of the accused and the public lack of understanding of the real problem.

In one midwestern city when prostitutes entered a commercial strip surrounded by a residential neighborhood, dozens of housewives and merchants carrying signs marched along the sidewalks, watching for cars that stopped to pick up prostitutes. The effectiveness of this grassroots campaign prompted the pimp to take his "team" out of the neighborhood, and the residents and merchants were able to score a real victory against this type of crime.

Prostitution can be prevented by

- public support of police efforts to arrest street prostitutes
- community awareness and organization to insist that these operations stay out of the neighborhood
- public awareness of the dangers of patronizing street prostitutes
- public pressure for stronger legislation affecting pimps

GAMBLING

Gambling on sporting events and games of chance has existed for a long time in this country—legally and illegally.

Many states have gambling boards and commissions to administer honest gambling operations. Betting at race tracks, legalized gambling at casinos, and off-track betting are allowed in many areas. By law, an honest count must be given, and the bettor must receive a fair return, based on the odds of his bet. Such gambling operations are legitimate.

Gambling not licensed by the state takes place on the streets, in factories, bars, and other places where people congregate. Any profits are unreported income for all involved. In such situations the odds may not be true, and the illegal operators create victims out of bettors and the community at large. Much of the huge profit from illegal gambling has been known to flow into other illegal activity and to support unscrupulous business people in our communities. The bettor who is not paid his due is a victim of illegal gambling. The community, which loses the taxes and licensing fees involved in a legitimate operation, is also a victim.

The so-called victimless crimes make victims of us all.

APPENDIXES

APPENDICES

APPENDIX A

VICTIMS' COMPENSATION PROGRAMS

In thirty-eight states and the District of Columbia innocent victims of violent crimes can apply for compensation for their losses. An individual applies to a specific state agency, usually called a victims' compensation board, which is funded by surcharges on court-imposed fines and the state's general revenue funds.

As the victim of a crime who has been physically injured, you are eligible to apply for compensation for your loss regardless of whether an arrest has been made. You may apply for compensation for your medical bills, lost wages, and other damages directly resulting from your injury. In the application process the administrators of the victims' compensation program may help you find additional sources of funds to compensate for your losses.

A surviving spouse, parent, child, or other family member of a victim who has died as a direct result of a crime may file for burial expenses and, in some states, for additional compensation. Good Samaritans—who are injured while endeavoring to help a crime victim—are also eligible.

A victim makes a claim by contacting the compensation board, obtaining the necessary forms, and filing those forms. A claim must be filed within a specified time period. A police report about the crime in question must also have been filed within a specified time period. Usually there is no requirement for an attorney or any filing fees. The time it takes to process a claim varies from state to state. In some instances emergency funds can be made available, but the amount provided will be deducted from the final amount of the award.

The total amount of compensation a victim may receive varies from $1,500 to $50,000. To ensure consideration of only the most serious crimes, some states have set a minimum amount that a victim can seek. In all thirty-eight states collateral sources of funds, such as medical insurance, are evaluated first.

A victim who has collected from a compensation board is not prevented from suing his attacker or instituting a third-party action. Rules vary from state to state as to whether a board will have a lien against additional proceeds a victim obtains.

If you are a victim you must take it upon yourself to seek out methods of compensation.

No formal victim compensation program has been established in the states of Alabama, Arizona, Arkansas, Idaho, Maine, Mississippi, New Hampshire, North Carolina,

South Dakota, Utah, Vermont, or Wyoming. Upon conviction, a defendant may be ordered by the judge to pay restitution. Many criminals, however, have no assets with which to satisfy such a charge.

The trend of compensating victims for their loss will encourage more states to establish formal restitution procedures through victim compensation programs administered by state-funded agencies.

Alaska

Agency: Violent Crimes Compensation Board
Department of Public Safety
450 Whittier Street
North Juno, Alaska 99811
907-465-3040

Type of crime: Specified violent crimes

*Time limit for
filing claim:* Two years from date of incident

*Time limit for
making police report:* Five days from date of incident

Usual processing time: Three to six months

Claim amount limits: Maximum: $40,000 if victim has multiple dependents; $25,000 for lone victim (victim with no dependents)

Filing fee: None

California

Agency:
State Board of Control, Victims of Crime Unit
926 J Street
Suite 300
Sacramento, California 95814
916-322-4426

Type of crime:
Misdemeanor or felony that produces injury

Time limit for filing claim:
One year from date of incident

Time limit for making police report:
As soon as possible

Usual processing time:
Six to eight months

Claim amount limits:
Maximum: $23,000; minimum: $100 or 20% of victim's net monthly income, whichever is less

Filing fee:
None

Colorado

Agency: Crime Victim Compensation Board (to be established)

Type of crime: Any compensable crime

Time limit for filing claim: Six months from date of incident

Time limit for making police report: Seventy-two hours from time of incident

Usual processing time: Unknown

Claim amount limits: Maximum: $1,500; minimum: $25

Filing fee: None

Connecticut

Agency: Criminal Injuries Compensation Board
101 Lafayette Street
Hartford, Connecticut 06106
203-566-4156

Type of crime: Misdemeanor or felony

*Time limit for
filing claim:* Two years from date of incident

*Time limit for
making police report:* Five days from date of incident

Usual processing time: Two months to one year

Claim amount limits: Maximum: $10,000; minimum: $100

Filing fee: None

Delaware

Agency: Delaware Violent Crimes Compensation Board
800 Delaware Avenue
Suite 500
Wilmington, Delaware 19801
302-571-3030

Type of crime: Any violent crime resulting in physical injury

Time limit for
filing claim: One year from date of incident

Time limit for
making police report: As soon as possible

Usual processing time: Four to eighteen months

Claim amount limits: Maximum: $10,000; minimum: $25

Filing fee: None

District of Columbia

Agency:

Office of Crime Victim Compensation Program
500 C Street
Washington, D.C. 20001
202-639-1211

Type of crime:

Violent crime

*Time limit for
filing a claim:*

Six months from date of incident

*Time limit for
making police report:*

Seven days from date of incident

Usual processing time:

Unknown

Claim amount limits:

Maximum: $25,000; minimum: $100

Filing fee:

$5

Florida

Agency:

Bureau of Crimes Compensation
2551 Executive Center Circle West
Lafayette Building
Suite 202
Tallahassee, Florida 32301
904-488-0848

Type of crime:

Any crime resulting in physical injury

*Time limit for
filing claim:*

One year from date of incident

*Time limit for
making police report:*

Seventy-two hours from time of incident

Usual processing time:

Three to four months

Claim amount limits:

Maximum: $10,000

Filing fee:

None

Georgia

Agency:

Claims Advisory Board
214 State Capitol
Atlanta, Georgia 30334
404-656-2899

Type of crime:

Any crime that results in injury to intervener

*Time limit for
filing a claim:*

By the November 15th following the incident

*Time limit for
making police report:*

By the November 15th following the incident

Usual processing time:

Three months to one year

Claim amount limits:

Maximum: $5,000

Filing fee:

None

Hawaii

Agency: Criminal Injuries Compensation Commission
Bethel-Pauahi Building, Room 412
1149 Bethel Street
Honolulu, Hawaii 96813
808-548-4680

Type of crime: Specified crimes that result in personal injury

*Time limit for
filing a claim:* Eighteen months from date of incident

*Time limit for
making police report:* Forty-eight hours from time of incident

Usual processing time: Six months

Claim amount limits: Maximum: $10,000

Filing fee: None

Illinois

Agency: The Attorney General Crime Victims Program
188 West Randolph Street, Room 2200
Chicago, Illinois 60601
312-793-2585

Type of crime: Any crime resulting in physical injury

*Time limit for
filing a claim:* Six months from date of incident to file a notice of intent; one year from date of incident to file application

*Time limit for
making police report:* Seventy-two hours from time of incident

Usual processing time: Six months to one year

Claim amount limits: Maximum: $15,000; minimum: $200

Filing fee: None

Indiana

Agency: Victims Violent Crimes Compensation Division
601 State Office Building
100 North Senate
Indianapolis, Indiana 46204
317-232-7103

Type of crime: Class A misdemeanor or felony

*Time limit for
filing claim:*   Ninety days from date of incident

*Time limit for
making police report*   Forty-eight hours from time of incident

Usual processing time: One to six months

Claim amount limits: Maximum: $10,000; minimum: $100

Filing fee: None

Iowa

Agency: Crime Victim Reparation Program
Wallace State Office Building
Des Moines, Iowa 50319
515-281-5044

Type of crime: Misdemeanor or felony

Time limit for filing a claim: Six months from date of incident for injury; four months from date of incident for death

Time limit for making police report: Twenty-four hours from time of incident

Usual processing time: Unknown

Claim amount limits: Maximum: $2,000

Filing fee: None

Kansas

Agency: Crime Victims Reparation Board
503 Kansas Avenue,
Suite 343
Topeka, Kansas 66603
913-269-2359

Type of crime: Violent crime

*Time limit for
filing a claim:* One year from date of incident

*Time limit for
making police report:* Seventy-two hours from time of incident

Usual processing time: Three to four months

Claim amount limits: Maximum: $10,000; minimum: $100

Filing fee: None

Kentucky

Agency:

Crime Victims Compensation Board
113 East Third Street
Frankfurt, Kentucky 40601
502-564-2290

Type of crime:

Criminal assault

*Time limit for
filing a claim:*

One year from date of incident

*Time limit for
making police report:*

Forty-eight hours from time of incident

Usual processing time:

Three to six months

Claim amount limits:

Maximum: $15,000; minimum: $100

Filing fee:

None

Louisiana

Agency:

Crime Victim Reparation,
Department of Correction
P.O. Box 44304
Baton Rouge, Louisiana 70804
501-342-6609

Type of crime: Misdemeanor or felony

*Time limit for
filing a claim:* One year from date of incident

*Time limit for
making police report:* Seventy-two hours from time of incident

Usual processing time: Unknown

Claim amount limits: Maximum: $10,000; minimum: $250

Filing fee: None

Maryland

Agency:
Criminal Injuries Compensation Board
1123 North Eutaw Street
Baltimore, Maryland 21201
301-523-5000

Type of crime:
Misdemeanor or felony

Time limit for filing a claim:
Six months from date of incident

Time limit for making police report:
Forty-eight hours from time of incident

Usual processing time:
One year

Claim amount limits:
Maximum: $45,000; minimum: $100 or two weeks' wages for victim, whichever is less

Filing fee:
None

Massachusetts

Agency: Victims of Violent Crime Compensation
                        1 Ashburton Place
                        Boston, Massachusetts 02108
                        617-727-5025

Type of crime: Any violent crime

*Time limit for
filing a claim:*   One year from date of incident for injuries; ninety days
                        from date of incident for death

*Time limit for
making police report:* Forty-eight hours from time of incident

Usual processing time: Six months

Claim amount limits: Maximum: $10,000; minimum: $100

Filing fee: $5

Michigan

Agency: Crime Victims Compensation Board
The Plaza Hotel
111 South Capitol,
Suite 808
Lansing, Michigan 48933
313-373-7373

Type of crime: Any crime resulting in personal injury

*Time limit for
filing a claim:* Thirty days from date of incident for injuries; ninety days from date of incident for death

*Time limit for
making police report:* Forty-eight hours from time of incident

Usual processing time: Four to twelve weeks

Claim amount limits: Maximum: $15,000; minimum: $100

Filing fee: None

Minnesota

Agency:

Minnesota Crime Victims Reparation Board
702 American Center Building
160 East Kellogg Boulevard
St. Paul, Minnesota 55501
612-296-7080

Type of crime:

Misdemeanor or felony

*Time limit for
filing a claim:*

One year from date of incident

*Time limit for
making police report:*

Five days from date of incident

Usual processing time:

Three months to one year

Claim amount limits:

Maximum: $25,000; minimum: $100

Filing fee:

None

Missouri

Agency:
Division of Workers Compensation
Crime Victim Unit
722 Jefferson
Jefferson City, Missouri 65101
314-751-4231

Type of crime:
Any violent crime

Time limit for filing a claim:
One year from date of incident for injuries; ninety days from date of incident for death

Time limit for making police report:
Forty-eight hours from time of incident

Usual processing time:
Unknown

Claim amount limits:
Maximum: $10,000; minimum: $200

Filing fee:
Undetermined

Montana

Agency:

Crime Victims Unit
Division of Workers' Compensation
815 Front Street
Helena, Montana 59601
406-449-5633

Type of crime:

Misdemeanor or felony

*Time limit for
filing a claim:*

One year from date of incident

*Time limit for
making police report:*

Seventy-two hours from time of incident

Usual processing time:

Twenty-eight to forty-seven days

Claim amount limits:

Maximum: $25,000 if employed at time of injury;
$20,000 if unemployed but employable

Filing fee:

None

Nebraska

Agency:
Nebraska Crime Victims' Reparation Board
Nebraska State Office Building
301 Centennial Mall South
Lincoln, Nebraska 68509
402-471-2828 or 402-471-2194

Type of crime:
Misdemeanor or felony

*Time limit for
filing a claim:*
Two years from date of incident

*Time limit for
making police report:*
Three days from date of incident

Usual processing time:
One to two months

Claim amount limits:
Maximum: $10,000

Filing fee:
None

Nevada

Agency: State Board of Examiners
                                     Supreme Court Building
                                     Carson City, Nevada 89710
                                     702-885-5670

Type of crime: Misdemeanor or felony

*Time limit for
filing a claim:*   Two years from date of incident

*Time limit for
making police report:*   Five days from date of incident

Usual processing time: Six months to one year

Claim amount limits: Maximum: $5,000; minimum: $100

Filing fee: None

New Jersey

Agency:

Violent Crimes Compensation Board
60 Park Place
Newark, New Jersey 07102
201-648-2107

Type of crime:

Misdemeanor or felony

*Time limit for
filing a claim:*

Two years from date of incident

*Time limit for
making police report:*

Three months from date of incident

Usual processing time:

Eighteen months to two years

Claim amount limits:

Maximum: $10,000; minimum: $100 or two weeks' wages for victim, whichever is less

Filing fee:

None

New Mexico

Agency: New Mexico Crime Victims Reparations Commission
8100 Mountain Road North East,
Suite 110
Albuquerque, New Mexico 87110
505-842-3907

Type of crime: Misdemeanor or felony

*Time limit for
filing a claim:* One year from date of incident

*Time limit for
making police report:* Thirty days from date of incident

Usual processing time: One to three months

Claim amount limits: Maximum: $12,500

Filing fee: None

New York

Agency:

Crime Victim Board
875 Central Avenue
Albany, New York 12206
518-457-1193

Type of crime: Any crime that produces personal injury

*Time limit for
filing a claim:* One year from date of incident

*Time limit for
making police report:* Within one week from date of incident

Usual processing time: One year

Claim amount limits: Maximum: $20,000

Filing fee: None

North Dakota

Agency:

North Dakota Crime Victims Reparations
Workmen's Compensation Bureau
Highway 83 North
Russell Building
Bismarck, North Dakota 58505
701-224-4151

Type of crime:

Any violent crime resulting in bodily injury

*Time limit for
filing a claim:*

One year from date of incident

*Time limit for
making police report:*

Seventy-two hours from time of incident

Usual processing time:

Six weeks

Claim amount limits:

Maximum: $25,000; minimum: $100

Filing fee:

None

Ohio

Agency: Victims of Crimes Division Program
Court of Claims
255 East Main Street
Columbus, Ohio 43215
614-466-6480

Type of crime: Misdemeanor or felony resulting in injury

*Time limit for
filing a claim:* One year from date of incident

*Time limit for
making police report:* Seventy-two hours from time of incident

Usual processing time: Six months to one year

Claim amount limits: Maximum: $50,000

Filing fee: $7.50

Oklahoma

Agency: Oklahoma Crime Victims' Compensation Board
3033 N. Walnut
Suite 101 West
Oklahoma City, Oklahoma 73105
405-521-2330

Type of crime: Misdemeanor or felony resulting in injury

*Time limit for
filing a claim:* One year from date of incident

*Time limit for
making police report:* Seventy-two hours from time of incident

Usual processing time: Fifty-four days

Claim amount limits: Maximum: $10,000

Filing fee: None

Oregon

Agency:

Crime Victim Compensation Fund
Dept. of Justice, State of Oregon
100 State Office Building
Salem, Oregon 97310
503-378-5348

Type of crime:

Any crime resulting in physical injury

*Time limit for
filing a claim:*

Six months from date of incident

*Time limit for
making police report:*

Seventy-two hours from time of incident

Usual processing time:

Sixty days

Claim amount limits:

Maximum: $23,000; minimum: $250

Filing fee:

None

Pennsylvania

Agency: Crime Victim Compensation Board
                                   1432 Strawberry Square
                                   Harrisburg, Pennsylvania 17120
                                   717-783-5153

Type of crime: Any violent crime

*Time limit for
filing a claim:*   One year from date of incident

*Time limit for
making police report:*   Seventy-two hours from time of incident

Usual processing time: One year

Claim amount limits: Maximum: $25,000; minimum: $100 or two weeks of
                                   victim's lost wages, whichever is less

Filing fee: None

Rhode Island

Agency:
Chief Clerk of Superior Court
State of Rhode Island
Superior Court
250 Benifit Street
Providence, Rhode Island 02901
401-277-3230

Type of crime:
Misdemeanor or felony

*Time limit for
filing a claim:*
Two years from date of incident; a lawyer is necessary;
fee determined by judge

*Time limit for
making police report:*
Must only be reported to police

Usual processing time:
Six months to one year

Claim amount limits:
Maximum: $25,000

Filing fee:
$25

South Carolina

Agency:

South Carolina Crime Victims' Compensation Fund
800 Dutch Square Building
Suite 160
Columbia, South Carolina 29210
803-758-2453

Type of crime:

Violent crime resulting in physical injury or death

*Time limit for
filing a claim:*

180 days from date of incident

*Time limit for
making police report:*

Forty-eight hours from time of incident

Usual processing time:

90 days

Claim amount limits:

Maximum: $10,000; minimum: $300 or two weeks'
wages for victim, whichever is less

Filing fee:

None

Tennessee

Agency:
State of Tennessee Board of Claims
1206 Andrew Jackson Boulevard
Nashville, Tennessee 37219
615-741-2734

Type of crime:
Any violent crime resulting in personal injury

Time limit for filing a claim:
One year from date of incident; a lawyer is needed, fee paid by state up to 15 percent of award amount

Time limit for making police report:
Forty-eight hours from time of incident

Usual processing time:
Six months to two years

Claim amount limits:
Maximum: $10,000; minimum $100 or two weeks' wages for victim, whichever is less

Filing fee:
Varies among counties

Texas

Agency:
Crime Victim Compensation Division
Texas Industrial Accident Board
200 East Riverside Drive
Austin, Texas 78764
512-475-8362

Type of crime:
Misdemeanor or felony resulting in physical or mental trauma

*Time limit for
filing a claim:*
Six months from date of incident

*Time limit for
making police report:*
Seventy-two hours from time of incident

Usual processing time:
Unknown

Claim amount limits:
Maximum: $50,000

Filing fee:
None

Virginia

Agency: Division of Crime Victims' Compensation
Industrial Commission of Virginia
P.O. Box 1794
Richmond, Virginia 23214
804-786-5171

Type of crime: Misdemeanor or felony

*Time limit for
filing a claim:* Six months from date of incident

*Time limit for
making police report:* Forty-eight hours from time of incident

Usual processing time: Three months

Claim amount limits: Maximum: $10,000; minimum: $100

Filing fee: None

Washington

Agency: Criminal Victims Compensation Section
Dept. of Labor and Industries
300 West Harrison Street
Seattle, Washington 98119
206-464-6519

Type of crime: Any crime resulting in physical injury

*Time limit for
filing a claim:* One year from date of incident

*Time limit for
making police report:* Seventy-two hours from time of incident

Usual processing time: One to three months

Claim amount limits: Maximum: $15,000 plus unlimited medical coverage;
minimum: $200

Filing fee: None

West Virginia

Agency:

West Virginia Court of Claims
Crime Reparation Division
Room 4 Main Unit
Capitol Building
Charleston, West Virginia 25305
304-348-3471

Type of crime: Any crime resulting in personal injury

*Time limit for
filing a claim:* Two years from date of incident

*Time limit for
making police report:* Seventy-two hours from time of incident

Usual processing time: Unknown

Claim amount limits: Maximum: $20,000

Filing fee: $10

Wisconsin

Agency:
Wisconsin Department of Justice
Crime Victim Compensation Program
123 West Washington Avenue
Madison, Wisconsin 53702
608-266-6470

Type of crime:
Misdemeanor or felony

*Time limit for
filing a claim:*
Two years from date of incident

*Time limit for
making police report:*
Five days from date of incident

Usual processing time:
Three months

Claim amount limits:
Maximum: $12,000

Filing fee:
None

APPENDIX B

RAPE CRISIS SERVICE— 24-HOUR HOTLINES

Selected rape crisis service hotlines are listed here. Many more exist throughout the country and are helpful and beneficial. If you do not find a listing for your area, call the nearest hotline listed and request the number for your area or check your directory. This listing is not an endorsement of any specific agency.

Alabama

Birmingham
Rape Response Program
205-323-7273

Montgomery
Council Against Rape Lighthouse
205-264-7273

Alaska

Anchorage
Standing Together Against Rape
907-276-7273

Fairbanks
Women in Crisis—Counseling and Assistance, Inc.
907-452-6770

Arizona

Phoenix
Center Against Sexual Assault
602-257-8095

Tucson
Tucson Rape Crisis Center, Inc.
602-623-7273

Arkansas

Little Rock

Rape Crisis, Inc.
501-375-5181

California

Berkeley

Bay Area Women Against Rape
415-845-7273

Fresno

Rape Counseling Service of Fresno, Inc.
209-222-7273

Irvine

Irvine Community Against Rape Everywhere
714-831-9110

Laguna Beach

Laguna Beach Free Clinic Rape Crisis Unit
714-494-0761

Long Beach

Long Beach Rape Hotline
213-545-2111

Los Angeles

Center for the Pacific-Asian Family
Pacific-Asian Rape Care-Line
213-653-4042

Los Angeles
(cont'd)

East Los Angeles Rape Crisis Center, Inc.
213-262-0944 (bilingual hotline)

Rape Response Service
213-855-3506

Greater Los Angeles

Emergency Rape Number
213-383-6919

Monterey

Rape Crisis Center of the Monterey Peninsula
408-375-4357

Orange

Orange County Rape Crisis Hotline
714-831-9110

Pasadena

Rape Emergency Assistance Crisis Telephone
213-793-3385

Sacramento

Sacramento Rape Crisis Center
916-447-7273

San Diego

Rape Crisis
714-233-3088

San Francisco

San Francisco Women Against Rape
415-647-7273

San Francisco (cont'd)	Sexual Trauma Services 415-558-3824
San Rafael	Marin Rape Crisis Center 415-924-2100
Santa Rosa	Rape Crisis Center of Sonoma County 707-545-7273
Stockton	Rape Crisis Center of San Joaquin County 209-465-4997

Colorado

Colorado Springs	Rape Crisis Service 303-633-3819
Denver	Rape Crisis Program 303-893-6000
	Battered Women 303-893-6111

Connecticut

Bridgeport
Rape Crisis Service
203-333-2233

Hartford
Sexual Assault Crisis Service/YWCA
203-522-6666

New Haven
Rape Counseling Team
203-436-1960

Stamford
Rape Crisis Service of Stamford
203-329-2929

Delaware

Wilmington
Rape Crisis Center of Wilmington
302-658-5011

District of Columbia

Washington, D.C.
FACT Hotline (Families and Children in Trouble)
202-628-3228

Florida

Daytona Beach   Victim Advocate Program and Investigation Unit
                     904-255-1931

Fort Lauderdale   Victim Advocate Office
                     305-761-2143

Jacksonville   Rape Crisis Center
                     904-354-3114

West Palm Beach   Sexual Assault Assistance Project
                     305-833-7273

Georgia

Atlanta   Rape Crisis Center
                     404-659-7273

Savannah   Rape Crisis Center of the Coastal Empire, Inc.
                     912-233-7273

Hawaii

Honolulu   Sex Abuse Treatment Center
                     808-524-7273

Idaho

Boise
Rape Crisis Alliance
208-345-7273

Rupert
Magic Valley Rape Crisis Center
208-436-3406

Illinois

Greater Chicago
Rape Crisis Emergency
312-744-8418

Chicago
Rape Victim Advocates
312-883-5688

Push for Excellence
312-373-3366

Springfield
Rape Information and Counseling Service (RICS)
217-753-8081

Indiana

Evansville
Citizens Against Rape in Evansville (C.A.R.E.)
812-425-4355

Fort Wayne

Rape Crisis Center, Inc.
219-426-7273

Indianapolis

Crisis Intervention Service
317-353-5947

Iowa

Ames

Story County Sexual Assault Center
515-292-1101

Iowa City

Rape Victim Advocacy Program
319-338-4800

Kansas

Manhattan

North Central Kansas Guidance Center
913-539-5337

Regional Crisis Center for Victims of Family Abuse or Rape
913-539-2785

Wichita

Wichita Area Rape Center, Inc.
316-263-3002

Kentucky

Louisville

R.A.P.E. Relief Center
502-581-7273

Louisiana

Baton Rouge

Stop Rape Crisis Center
504-383-7273

New Orleans

YWCA Rape Crisis Service
504-821-6000

Maine

Portland

Rape Crisis Center of Greater Portland
207-774-3613

Maryland

Annapolis

Anne Arundel County Sexual Offense Crisis Center
301-224-1321

Baltimore   Baltimore Center for Victims of Sexual Assault
                   301-366-7273

Bethesda   Community Crisis Center
                   301-656-9161

Massachusetts

Boston   Project Place
                   617-267-9150

                   Rape Crisis Intervention Program
                   617-735-2000

                   Rape Investigation Unit
                   617-247-4400

Cambridge   Boston Area Rape Crisis Center
                   617-492-7273

Hyannis   Mid Cape Rape Crisis Unit
                   617-771-1080

Springfield   Hotline to End Rape and Abuse (HERA)
                   413-733-2561

Michigan

Ann Arbor
Assault Crisis Center
313-994-1616

Detroit
Detroit Central City Community Mental Health Center
313-831-3160

Flint
Sexual Assault Crisis Center
313-238-7233

Grand Rapids
Rape Crisis Team
616-774-3535

Minnesota

Duluth
Aid to Victims of Sexual Assault
218-727-8538

Minneapolis
Rape and Sexual Assault Center
612-825-4357

St. Paul
Sexual Offense Services of Ramsey County (S.O.S.)
612-298-5898

Mississippi

Jackson

No hotline available; contact State Police
601-982-1212

Missouri

Kansas City

Sexual Assault Treatment Center
816-923-1123

St. Louis

Rape Crisis Center
314-725-2010

Montana

Kalispell

Kalispell Rape Crisis Line
406-755-5067

Missoula

Women's Resource Center
406-243-4153

Nebraska

Omaha

Women Against Violence
402-345-7273

Nevada

Las Vegas   Community Action Against Rape
                 702-735-1111

New Hampshire

Manchester   Women's Crisis Line for Rape Victims and Battered Women
                 603-668-2299

New Jersey

Atlantic City   Atlantic County Prosecutor's Office
                 609-345-6700

                 Women's Center Hotline
                 609-646-6767

Elizabeth   Union County Prosecutor's Office
                 201-654-4847

Hackensack   Sex Crimes/Child Abuse Unit
                 201-646-2300

Hackensack
(cont'd)

Women's Counseling and Psychotherapy Service
201-487-5070

New Mexico

Albuquerque

Albuquerque Rape Crisis Center
505-247-0707

Santa Fe

Santa Fe Rape Crisis Center, Inc.
505-982-4667

New York

Binghamton

Rape Crisis Center
607-722-4256

Bronx

Borough Crisis Center
212-579-5326, 579-5327, or 579-5328

Brooklyn

Borough Crisis Center
212-735-2424, 735-2425, or 735-2426

Buffalo

Anti-Rape Advocacy
716-834-3131

Manhattan

Borough Crisis Center
212-694-8251, 694-8252, or 694-8253
Victim Services Agency, Inc.—Hotline
212-577-7777

Rochester

Rape Crisis Service of Planned Parenthood of Rochester and
Monroe County
716-546-2595

Syracuse

Rape Crisis Center of Syracuse, Inc.
315-422-7273

White Plains

Bureau of Sex Crimes Analysis and Crisis Intervention
914-592-8400

North Carolina

Asheville

Rape Crisis Center of Asheville
704-255-7576

Chapel Hill

Chapel Hill-Carrboro Rape Crisis Center
919-967-7273

Winston-Salem

Winston Women Against Rape/Rape Line
919-722-5153

North Dakota

Fargo   Rape and Abuse Crisis Center of Fargo-Moorhead
701-293-7273

Ohio

Akron   Akron Rape Crisis Center
216-434-7273

Cincinnati   Women Helping Women, Inc.
513-381-5610

Columbus   Women Against Rape
614-221-4447

Oklahoma

Oklahoma City   YWCA Women's Resource Center—Rape Crisis
405-524-7273

Oregon

Oregon City   Clackamas County Rape Victim Advocate Program
503-655-8616

Pennsylvania

Erie
Erie County Rape Crisis Center
814-456-1001 and 868-1001

Harrisburg
Harrisburg Area Rape Crisis Center
717-238-7273

Philadelphia
Women Organized Against Rape
215-922-3434

Pittsburgh
Pittsburgh Against Rape
412-765-2731

Scranton
Rape Crisis Program at the Women's Resource Center
717-346-4671

Wilkes-Barre
Luzerne County Women Organized Against Rape
717-823-0765

Rhode Island

Providence
Rhode Island Rape Crisis Center, Inc.
401-941-2400

South Carolina

Charleston

People Against Rape
803-722-7273

South Dakota

Brookings

Rape Education, Advocacy and Counseling Team
605-688-4518 or emergency 911 (police)

Tennessee

Knoxville

Knoxville Rape Crisis Center
615-522-7273

Memphis

Comprehensive Rape Crisis Program
901-528-2161

Nashville

Rape and Sexual Abuse Center of Davidson County
615-327-1110

Texas

Austin

Austin Child Guidance Center
512-472-7273

Dallas   Dallas County Rape Crisis Center
              214-521-1020

Fort Worth   Rape Crisis Support of Tarrant County
              817-336-3355

Houston   Houston Rape Crisis Coalition
              713-228-1505

Utah

Provo   Timpanogos Community Mental Health Center
              801-373-7393

              Utah County Rape Crisis Line
              801-226-8989

Vermont

Burlington   Women's Rape Crisis Center
              802-863-1236

Rutland   Rutland County Rape Crisis Team
              802-775-1000

Virginia

Alexandria   Fairfax County Victim Assistance Network
703-360-7273

Richmond   Crisis Intervention Program
804-648-9224

Roanoke   TRUST, The Roanoke Valley Trouble Center
703-563-0311

Washington

Seattle   Crisis Clinic, Inc.
206-447-3222

Seattle Rape Relief
206-632-7273

Spokane   Rape Crisis Network
509-624-7273

West Virginia

Charleston
Sexual Assault Information Center, Inc.
304-344-9834

Wisconsin

Green Bay
Green Bay Rape Crisis Center, Ltd.
414-443-0584

Milwaukee
Women's Crisis Line
414-964-7535

Oshkosh
Winnebago County Rape Crisis Center
414-426-1460 and 233-7707

Racine
Women's Resource Center
414-633-3233

Wyoming

Jackson
Western Wyoming Mental Health Association
307-733-4870

GLOSSARY

accusatory instrument a factual document signed by a private person or a police officer that charges a person with a crime

adjournment rescheduling of a case for a future date

admissible evidence evidence acceptable in court as legal proof

admission of guilt a confession, as to a crime; words uttered by a speaker *against* his or her interest

affidavit a document signed under oath as to the truth of its contents

appeal a post-trial request, made to a higher court, for review of a case for modification or reversal of a lower court's decision

appearance ticket a notice given to a person who has been arrested that requires his or her appearance in court on a specific charge *arbitration* an alternative to a court process where a third person, not a judge, hears a dispute and makes a binding decision

arbitrator an impartial person who hears a dispute and renders a binding decision

arraignment the first personal appearance of a defendant in court on a specific charge and the entry of a plea of guilty or not guilty; the court's initial exercise of power over the defendant

arrest to place under custody in order to answer criminal charges in court

attorney general a state prosecutor

award a civil decision or result in favor of a claimant

bail money deposited with the court by a person accused of a crime to obtain his or her release from custody prior to the trial; it assures reappearance of the defendant in court at a future date

bail bond a written guarantee that a person will appear in court at the next court date; if the defendant fails to appear, the amount of cash in the bond must be paid to the court

bailiff an official of the court, usually in uniform, who is responsible for keeping order in the courtroom and assisting both the judge and the public

bar lawyers collectively; the legal profession

bench the seat occupied by the judge in the courtroom; also may refer to the court itself

beyond a reasonable doubt the standard of proof necessary for conviction of a person charged with a crime

case law rules of precedent, usually set by appeals

courts, that must be followed in subsequent legal matters

casualty injury, damage, or loss

civil law law dealing with disputes between individuals

claim a demand for something as one's rightful due

claimant a person bringing, or filing, a civil claim; a petitioner or plaintiff

compensation payment or reimbursement for a loss

conditional discharge a sentence setting up conditions that a convicted defendant, once released from custody, must obey for a period of time

confession a statement made admitting guilt

constable a civil enforcement officer who serves legal notices in attempts to collect awards

conviction a finding by a judge or jury that the person charged committed a crime

court attendant a uniformed official of the court, usually the judge's assistant, who keeps order in the court

court clerk the administrative officer in charge of the court office; assists the public in filing charges

court officer a court attendant, bailiff, civil enforcement officer

court reporter recorder of all words stated in court, who transcribes them if necessary

credibility the believability of something claimed or stated

crime an act prohibited by criminal law

criminal complaint an accusatory instrument filed with the court charging a person with violation of the criminal law *criminal law*   a set of written standards that, if violated, can result in arrest

cross-examination   questions challenging statements made under oath; usually conducted by defense attorney

custody   detention under the control of a law enforcement officer

defendant   in criminal law, a person charged with a crime; in civil law, a person against whom a claim is brought

defense   a denial of the validity or truth of a charge

defense attorney   the lawyer who represents a defendant

direct case   complete proof against a defendant that must prove a defendant guilty or the charge will be dismissed

direct testimony   statements made in person in open court

dismissal   termination of a criminal case because the people fail to provide adequate evidence to support the charge, or in a civil case, when the claimant fails to provide adequate evidence to support a claim, and it is determined that there is no cause for action

district attorney   a lawyer employed by the local government, in charge of prosecuting those accused of committing crimes

diversion   removal of a case from the criminal court for alternative settlement

felony   a crime for which the sentence may exceed one year

grand jury   group of citizens empaneled by the court to decide if criminal charges should be brought

hearsay   evidence that is not verifiable and not acceptable as proof *incriminate*   to indicate guilt by statement or proof

infraction   a minor non-criminal violation of law

judgment   a decision entered upon the official record of the court

jurisdiction   the power of the court to administer justice; the extent of a court's authority

jury   up to twelve members of the community who attend a criminal trial and determine guilt or innocence

jury trial   a process of presenting a case against an accused in the presence of a jury that will determine guilt or innocence

lawsuit   a case brought in court

liability   legal responsibility

lien   the right of a creditor to specific real or personal property of a debtor

lineup   an identification procedure used by the police whereby a victim or witness views a group of people for the purpose of identifying a suspect

litigate   to bring legal action in court

local criminal court   the court in which felony arraignments may take place and misdemeanor and petty offense trials are heard; a town, village, city, or municipal court

marshal   a civil enforcement officer of the court

mediation   the procedure by which parties are brought together in an attempt to resolve their dispute by arriving at a mutual decision

misdemeanor   a crime for which the sentence cannot exceed one year

motion   a request that the court rule on legal matters

municipal court   in many areas, the local criminal court

negligence actions resulting in injury or damage by carelessness, in which one may be legally responsible for compensating another person for injury or damage

oath a pledge to tell the truth

order of protection an order of the court directing a family member to refrain from offensive conduct; violation of this order could result in a person being placed in custody

party in civil law, a person who brings a claim or a person against whom a claim is brought

people the prosecution; the state; all criminal cases are prosecuted by the people

personal property tangible, physical goods such as cash, jewelry, bonds, stocks, and personal effects

petition a document signed by a person seeking relief from the court; in family court, the placing of a charge against a family member

petitioner one seeking relief from the court

petty offense a non-criminal violation of the criminal law

photo array an identification procedure used by police whereby a victim or witness views several photographs in an attempt to identify a suspect

physical evidence tangible, physical proof of a crime usually found at a crime scene

plaintiff the person initiating a charge in court

plea the admission or denial of a criminal charge; guilty or not guilty

preliminary hearing a proceeding before the trial of a criminal case

probation   a period during which a released convicted criminal must obey certain conditions set forth in the probation and report to a specific individual known as a probation officer

prosecutor   a lawyer who represents the people in prosecuting criminal cases

public defender   a lawyer who defends one charged with a crime at no cost because the defendant has no funds

release on recognizance   the release of a defendant from custody prior to his trial, for appearance at a subsequent court date, without the necessity of posting bail

respondent   the person against whom a claim is made; a defendant

restitution   payment that a victim receives for his loss

sheriff   a civil or criminal law enforcement officer

statute of limitations   the time limit within which a claim must be filed or a charge must be brought

statutory law   law passed by a legislative body and approved by the governor or executive and published in a code of laws

stenographer   the official court reporter who records in writing all of the words stated in court

subpoena   an order of the court requiring a person to appear before the court

sue   to bring legal action

superior court   the court in which felony trials are heard to completion

supporting deposition   a statement made under oath containing facts that tend to support statements made in an accusatory instrument

survivor   a person, often a relative of a victim, suffering
   a direct loss as the result of a victim's death

testimony   everything stated under oath

true bill   a charge made by a grand jury accusing a
   person of a felony

verdict   the decision of a jury as to guilt or innocence

victim   the person against whom a crime is committed

voir dire   the process of selecting a jury

witness   a person who has knowledge of facts pertaining
   to a case and subsequently takes an oath and testifies

witness stand   the chair in which the person who is tes-
   tifying sits

INDEX